TEACHER'S PET PUBLICATIONS

LITPLAN TEACHER PACK
for
A Day No Pigs Would Die
based on the book by
Robert Newton Peck

Written by
Barbara M. Linde, MA Ed.

© 1997 Teacher's Pet Publications
All Rights Reserved

This **LitPlan** for Robert Newton Peck's
A Day No Pigs Would Die
has been brought to you by Teacher's Pet Publications, Inc.

Copyright Teacher's Pet Publications 1997

Only the student materials in this unit plan (such as worksheets,
study questions, and tests) may be reproduced multiple times
for use in the purchaser's classroom.

For any additional copyright questions,
contact Teacher's Pet Publications.

www.tpet.com

TABLE OF CONTENTS *A Day No Pigs Would Die*

Introduction	5
Unit Objectives	7
Unit Outline	8
Reading Assignment Sheet	9
Study Questions	13
Quiz/Study Questions (Multiple Choice)	23
Pre-Reading Vocabulary Worksheets	41
Lesson One (Introductory Lesson)	57
Writing Assignment 1	63
Oral Reading Evaluation Form	69
Writing Assignment 2	71
Writing Evaluation Form	72
Nonfiction Assignment Sheet	76
Extra Writing Assignments/Discussion ?s	82
Writing Assignment 3	90
Vocabulary Review Activities	91
Unit Review Activities	92
Unit Tests	99
Unit Resource Materials	129
Vocabulary Resource Materials	143

A FEW NOTES ABOUT THE AUTHOR
ROBERT NEWTON PECK

PECK, ROBERT NEWTON, was born on February 17, 1928, in Vermont. Children, teenagers, and adults alike found his style irresistible, despite the realistic and sometimes gory descriptions of farm life in many of his books.

Peck received an A. B. degree from Rollins College in 1953 and studied law at Cornell University. He served in the U. S. Army from 1945 to 1947 and wrote his first book, *A Day No Pigs Would Die*, in 1973. The agony of the book's hero over having to butcher his pet pig contrasts with the seeming stability of the rural setting.

Peck published more than 20 other books in the 1970s, including a volume of poetry called *Bee Tree and Other Stuff* (1975.) His book *Soup and Me* (1975) was adapted for television's After School Special in 1978. It and his other books about the character Soup reflect the author's childhood on a farm in Vermont. He also wrote several historical novels, including *Rabbits and Redcoats*, (1976), which takes place at the Battle of Fort Ticonderoga, and a musical, *King of Kazoo* (1976), which was intended to be enacted by children.

Publications

A Day No Pigs Would Die, 1973	*Trig Goes Ape*, 1980
Path of Hunters 1973	*Soup on Wheels*, 1981
Millie's Boy, 1973	*Justice Lion*, 1981
Soup, 1974	*Trig or Treat*, 1982
Soup and Me, 1974	*Banjo*, 1982
Fawn, 1975	*Soup in the Saddle*, 1983
Wild Cat, 1975	*Seminole Seed*, 1983
Bee Tree and Other Stuff, (poems) 1975	*Dukes*, 1983
Hamilton, 1976	*Soup's Goat*, 1984
Hang for Treason, 1976	*Soup on Ice*, 1985
Rabbits and Redcoats, 1976	*Jo Silver*, 1985
King of Kazoo, (musical) 1976	*Hallapoosa*, 1985
Last Sunday, 1977	*Horse Hunters*, 1988
The King's Iron, 1977	*Soup on Fire*, 1987
Patooie, 1977	*Arly*, 1989
Soup for President, 1978	*Higbee's Halloween*, 1990
Eagle Fur, 1978	*Arly's Run*, 1991
Trig Sees Red, 1978	*Soup in Love*, 1992
Basket Case, 1979	*Little Soup's Birthday*, 1992
Hub, 1979	*Little Soup's Turkey*, 1992
Mr. Little, 1979	*Soup's Hoop*, 1993
Clunie, 1979	*A Part of the Sky* (sequel to A Day No Pigs), 1994
Soup's Drum, 1980	*Soup 1776*, 1995

Courtesy of Compton's Learning Company

INTRODUCTION

This unit has been designed to develop students' reading, writing, thinking, listening and speaking skills through exercises and activities related to *A Day No Pigs Would Die* by Robert Newton Peck. It includes twenty lessons, supported by extra resource materials.

The **introductory lesson** introduces students to Vermont farm life and the Shaker religion through a bulletin board activity. Following the introductory activity, students are given an explanation of how the activity relates to the book they are about to read.

The **reading assignments** are approximately twenty pages each; some are a little shorter while others are a little longer. Students have approximately 15 minutes of pre-reading work to do prior to each reading assignment. This pre-reading work involves reviewing the study questions for the assignment and doing some vocabulary work for 8 to 10 vocabulary words they will encounter in their reading.

The **study guide questions** are fact-based questions; students can find the answers to these questions right in the text. These questions come in two formats: short answer or multiple choice. The best use of these materials is probably to use the short answer version of the questions as study guides for students (since answers will be more complete), and to use the multiple choice version for occasional quizzes. It might be a good idea to make transparencies of your answer keys for the overhead projector.

The **vocabulary work** is intended to enrich students' vocabularies as well as to aid in the students' understanding of the book. Prior to each reading assignment, students will complete a two-part worksheet for approximately 8 to 10 vocabulary words in the upcoming reading assignment. Part I focuses on students' use of general knowledge and contextual clues by giving the sentence in which the word appears in the text. Students are then to write down what they think the words mean based on the words' usage. Part II gives students dictionary definitions of the words and has them match the words to the correct definitions based on the words' contextual usage. Students should then have an understanding of the words when they meet them in the text.

After each reading assignment, students will go back and formulate answers for the study guide questions. Discussion of these questions serves as a **review** of the most important events and ideas presented in the reading assignments.

After students complete extra discussion questions, there is a **vocabulary review** lesson which pulls together all of the separate vocabulary lists for the reading assignments and gives students a review of all of the words they have studied.

Following the reading of the book, two lessons are devoted to the **extra discussion questions/writing assignments**. These questions focus on interpretation, critical analysis and personal response, employing a variety of thinking skills and adding to the students' understanding of the novel. These questions are done as a **group activity**. Using the information they have acquired so far through individual work and class discussions, students get together to further examine the text and to brainstorm ideas relating to the themes of the novel.

The group activity is followed by a **reports and discussion** session in which the groups share their ideas about the book with the entire class; thus, the entire class gets exposed to many different ideas regarding the themes and events of the book.

There are three **writing assignments** in this unit, each with the purpose of informing, persuading, or having students express personal opinions. The first assignment is to express a **personal opinion**: students will complete written and illustrated journal entries to respond to each chapter. The second assignment is to inform: students will write an autobiography. The third assignment is to **persuade**: students will write a persuasive letter to an adult, either asking to get a pet or keep a pet that is in danger of being removed.

In addition, there is a **nonfiction reading assignment**. Students are required to read a piece of nonfiction related in some way to *A Day No Pigs Would Die*. After reading their nonfiction pieces, students will fill out a worksheet on which they answer questions regarding facts, interpretation, criticism, and personal opinions. During one class period, students make **oral presentations** about the nonfiction pieces they have read. This not only exposes all students to a wealth of information, it also gives students the opportunity to practice **public speaking**.

The **review lesson** pulls together all of the aspects of the unit. The teacher is given four or five choices of activities or games to use which all serve the same basic function of reviewing all of the information presented in the unit.

The **unit test** comes in two formats: all multiple choice-matching-true/false or with a mixture of matching, short answer, and composition. As a convenience, two different tests for each format have been included.

There are additional **support materials** included with this unit. The **resource sections** include suggestions for an in-class library, crossword and word search puzzles related to the novel, and extra vocabulary worksheets. There is a list of **bulletin board ideas** which gives the teacher suggestions for bulletin boards to go along with this unit. In addition, there is a list of **extra class activities** the teacher could choose from to enhance the unit or as a substitution for an exercise the teacher might feel is inappropriate for his/her class. **Answer keys** are located directly after the **reproducible student materials** throughout the unit. The student materials may be reproduced for use in the teacher's classroom without infringement of copyrights. No other portion of this unit may be reproduced without the written consent of Teacher's Pet Publications, Inc.

UNIT OBJECTIVES
A Day No Pigs Would Die

1. Through reading *A Day No Pigs Would Die* students will analyze characters and their situations to better understand the themes of the novel.

2. Students will demonstrate their understanding of the text on four levels: factual, interpretive, critical, and personal.

3. Students will practice reading aloud and silently to improve their skills in each area.

4. Students will enrich their vocabularies and improve their understanding of the novel through the vocabulary lessons prepared for use in conjunction with it.

5. Students will answer questions to demonstrate their knowledge and understanding of the main events   and characters in *A Day No Pigs Would Die*.

6. Students will practice writing through a variety of writing assignments.

7. The writing assignments in this are geared to several purposes:
	a. To check the students' reading comprehension
	b. To make students think about the ideas presented by the novel
	c. To make students put those ideas into perspective
	d. To encourage critical and logical thinking
	e. To provide the opportunity to practice good grammar and improve students' use of the English language.

8. Students will read aloud, report, and participate in large and small group discussions to improve their public speaking and personal interaction skills.

UNIT OUTLINE
A Day No Pigs Would Die

1 Unit Intro Distribute Unit Materials PV 1-2	2 R 1-2 Writing Assignment #1 Personal Opinion	3 ?? 1-2 Minilesson: Figurative Language	4 PVR 3-4 Oral Reading Evaluation	5 ?? 3-4 PVR 5-6
6 Writing Assignment #2 Inform	7 ?? 5-6 PVR 7-8	8 ??7-8 Quiz Nonfiction Assignment	9 PVR 9-10 Minilesson: Story Map	10 ?? 9-10 PVR 11-12
11 ?? 11-12 PVR 13-15	12 ?? 13-15 Minilesson: Character Development	13 Writing Conferences	14 Extra Discussion ??	15 Projects
16 Writing Assignment #3 Persuade	17 Vocabulary Review	18 Unit Review	19 Test	20 Nonfiction Assignment Presentations

Key: P = Preview Study Questions   V = Vocabulary Work   R = Read

READING ASSIGNMENT SHEET
A Day No Pigs Would Die

Date to be Assigned	Chapters	Completion Date
		(Prior to class on this date)
	Chapters 1-2	
	Chapters 3-4	
	Chapters 5-6	
	Chapters 7-8	
	Chapters 9-10	
	Chapters 11-12	
	Chapters 13-15	

STUDY QUESTIONS

SHORT ANSWER STUDY QUESTIONS *A Day No Pigs Would Die*

Chapters 1-2
1. Why did the narrator hate Edward Thatcher?
2. What was the first problem the narrator noticed with Apron? How did he help her? (List the things he did, in order.)
3. What was the second problem the narrator noticed with Apron? How did he help her? (List the steps in order.)
4. What was the narrator's name? What was his father's name?
5. Who found Rob?
6. Describe Rob's condition, and what his parents did to help him.
7. What was Haven Peck's occupation?
8. When did Rob think his father smelled the best, and why?

Chapters 3-4
1. Describe the "odd parade" Rob and his father saw.
2. What did Mr. Tanner give Rob, and why?
3. Mr. Peck did not want to accept a gift just for being a good neighbor. How did Mr. Tanner get him to accept the gift?
4. What did Rob name his pet?
5. Rob said he disagreed with his father about one Shaker law in particular. What was it? Why did he disagree?
6. Could Mr. Peck vote? If not, why not?
7. What did Mr. Peck say his mission was?
8. What, according to Mr. Peck, made Vermont a good state?
9. How did Rob feel the first night he had Pinky?

Chapters 5-6
1. What, according to Rob, was the best part of Shaker Meeting?
2. How did Mr. Tanner's farm look, compared to the Peck farm?
3. After whom was Rob named? Why was this person famous?
4. Why did Mama call Rob to the barn?
5. How big was Pinky by June?
6. Who was at the house visiting?
7. What was Robert's big mistake? What happened as a result of his mistake?
8. Aunt Matty had a reason for Rob's D in English. What was it?
9. What was Aunt Matte's job before she married Uncle Hue?
10. What was the reason, according to Aunt Matty, that Rob didn't know grammar?

Study Questions *A Day No Pigs Would Die* Page 2

Chapters 7-8
1. What did the hawk catch?
2. Did Rob know the amount of food Pinky was eating?
3. What did Rob intend to do with Pinky?
4. What was Rob's favorite sight?
5. Who came to the house during the thunderstorm, and why?
6. Who was Letty Phelps? What happened to her?
7. What did Haven Peck do when he found Sebring Hillman?
8. What did Mr. Hillman want to do with the smaller coffin? Why?

Chapters 9-10
1. What did Aunt Carrie think was shameful? What was Mama's opinion on the subject?
2. Summarize Rob's first run-in with the Widow Bascom.
3. Summarize Rob's second run-in with the Widow Bascom.
4. How did Rob get the opportunity to go to the Rutland Fair?
5. How did Mama and Aunt Carrie feel about Rob going to Rutland?
6. What did Rob tell Pinky about the Widow Bascom?
7. What one word did Papa say as Rob got out of the wagon at the Tanners' house?
8. List, in order, the things Rob did when he got to the fair.
9. Did Pinky win a prize? If so, what was it?

Chapters 11-12
1. Did Rob tell his parents that he got sick at the fair?
2. How did Rob feel about going to the fair?
3. What happened when Ira Long, Rob, and Papa tried to weasel Ira's dog, Hussy?
4. What problem did Papa think there might be with Pinky?
5. Did Haven Peck want Rob to be just like him when he grew up?
6. What did Mr. Tanner say about Mr. Peck?
7. Rob said he wanted a store-bought, red and black plaid coat. What was Papa's response?
8. What did Papa tell Rob while they were sitting by the fire in the parlor?

Study Questions *A Day No Pigs Would Die* Page 3

Chapters 13-15
1. Mr. Tanner asked Rob about Haven Peck's health. What was Rob's answer?
2. What did Mr. Tanner think of farming?
3. What religion were Mr. and Mrs. Tanner?
4. How was the apple crop?
5. What happened to Pinky, and why?
6. What did Rob say he wanted to do? What did he do?
7. Which day was the day no pigs would die? Why?
8. What did Rob find in the cigar box under his father's tools?
9. What did Rob do after he sent his mother and Aunt Carrie to bed with cups of hot tea?

ANSWER KEY: SHORT ANSWER STUDY QUESTIONS
A Day No Pigs Would Die

Chapters 1-2
1. Why did the narrator hate Edward Thatcher?
    Edward had made fun of the narrator's clothes and Shaker ways.

2. What was the first problem the narrator noticed with Apron? How did he help her? (List the things he did, in order.)
    Apron was a Holstein cow who was trying to give birth, but the calf was stuck. The narrator took off his pants and tied one leg around the calf's head. Apron started running again, and he followed her. When she stopped, he tied the other pants leg to a tree. Then he hit and stoned Apron until she started forward, which finally made the calf come out.

3. What was the second problem the narrator noticed with Apron? How did he help her? (List the steps in order.)
    Apron could not breathe. He put his hand down into her throat and felt a hard ball. He pulled on it. The cow bit the narrator's arm and started running. Then the narrator blacked out.

4. What was the narrator's name? What was his father's name?
    The narrator was Robert Peck (also the author.) The father was Haven Peck.

5. Who found Rob?
    Benjamin Tanner, a neighbor, and the owner of the cow, found Robert.

6. Describe Rob's condition, and what his parents did to help him.
    He was very bloody. His father pulled the blanket away from his bloody shoulder. His mother sewed up his arm. Then his parents put Robert to bed.

7. What was Haven Peck's occupation?
    He was a pig butcher.

8. When did Rob think his father smelled the best, and why?
    He smelled the best on Sunday morning, because he had taken a bath on Saturday night and washed the pig smells off. On Sunday he smelled like soap.

Chapters 3-4

1. Describe the "odd parade" Rob and his father saw.
    It consisted of Mr. Tanner, Apron, and her two calves. The calves were trying to get milk from Apron as they walked. Mr. Tanner has something under his arm.

2. What did Mr. Tanner give Rob, and why?
    Mr. Tanner gave Rob a piglet. It was a gift of thanks for delivering Apron's calf.

3. Mr. Peck did not want to accept a gift just for being a good neighbor. How did Mr. Tanner get him to accept the gift?
    First, Mr. Tanner asked when Rob's birthday was, then offered the piglet as a late birthday present. Mr. Peck was not comfortable with this. Then Mr. Tanner asked Mr. Peck to help him yoke the two calves the following fall. Mr. Peck agreed and Mr. Tanner offered the piglet as payment. Mr. Peck agreed to this arrangement.

4. What did Rob name his pet?
    He named the piglet Pinky.

5. Rob said he disagreed with his father about one Shaker law in particular. What was it? Why did he disagree?
    He disagreed with the law that said they could not go to baseball games on Sunday. He thought since he would only be watching, it should be acceptable. He wanted to see the Greemobys play.

6. Could Mr. Peck vote? If not, why not?
    No, he couldn't vote, because he couldn't read or write.

7. What did Mr. Peck say his mission was?
    He said he mission was killing pigs.

8. What, according to Mr. Peck, made Vermont a good state?
    The people of Vermont knew they could turn grass into milk and corn into hogs.

9. How did Robert feel the first night he had Pinky?
    He thought he was the luckiest boy in Learning.

Chapters 5-6

1. What, according to Rob, was the best part of Shaker Meeting?
    He sat where he could see Becky Tate but she could not see him.

2. How did Mr. Tanner's farm look, compared to the Peck farm?
    It looked prosperous.

3. After whom was Rob named? Why was this person famous?
    He was named after Major Robert Roger. He was famous because he had done a lot with the Indians. Some of the people thought he was a Shaker.

4. Why did Mama call Rob to the barn?
    She wanted to show him the cat, Miss Sarah, and her new kittens.

5. How big was Pinky by June?
    She was as big as Rob.

6. Who was at the house visiting?
    Aunt Matty was there. She visited once a month.

7. What was Robert's big mistake? What happened as a result of his mistake?
    He showed his report card to his mother, Aunt Carrie, and Aunt Matty. His mother and Aunt Carrie could not read. All they noticed was the A's. They both said Rob was a good boy. However, Aunt Matty could read and she saw the D in English. She offered to tutor Rob.

8. Aunt Matty had a reason for Rob's D in English. What was it?
    She said the D was due to his Shaker upbringing. She said if he were a fearing Baptist he would have a better grade.

9. What was Aunt Matty's job before she married Uncle Hue?
    She was an English teacher.

10. What was the reason, according to Aunt Matty, that Rob didn't know grammar?
    He didn't know how to diagram sentences.

Chapters 7-8

1. What did the hawk catch?
   It caught a cottontail rabbit.

2. Did Rob know the amount of food Pinky was eating?
   Yes, he kept a record of how much he fed Pinky.

3. What did Rob intend to do with Pinky?
   He wanted her to be a brood sow.

4. What was Rob's favorite sight?
   It was the heavens at sundown.

5. Who came to the house during the thunderstorm, and why?
   Mrs. Hillman came to the house. Her husband, Sebring, had gone to a grave to desecrate it.

6. Who was Letty Phelps? What happened to her?
   Letty was a relative of Haven Peck's. She got pregnant by Sebring Hillman. She drowned the baby, then hung herself.

7. What did Haven Peck do when he found Sebring Hillman?
   He had his gun with him, but said it was for varmints, not neighbors. He helped Sebring dig in the earth and find the smaller coffin. He agreed with Sebring's decision about burying the child. Then he suggested Mr. Hillman ride with them, since they had a slicker. He drove them all home for breakfast.

8. What did Mr. Hillman want to do with the smaller coffin? Why?
   He wanted to give the dead child his name, because it was his child. He regretted not admitting that when Letty was alive. Then he wanted to bury the child in his plot.

Chapters 9-10

1. What did Aunt Carrie think was shameful? What was Mama's opinion on the subject?
   Aunt Carrie thought it was shameful that the Widow Bascom and her hired man were living together. She was upset because another friend, Hume, had heard the two of them giggling in the dark. Mama said the Bascom place looked good, and a widow could not run a farm alone. She said the Widow Bascom and the hired man could have her blessing if they were giggling in the dark.

2. Summarize Rob's first run-in with the Widow Bascom.
   The run-in happened after Vernal Bascom had died. Rob and a friend, Jacob Henry, had run through her strawberry patch and across her backyard. She whacked both of them with a broom.

3. Summarize Rob's second run-in with the Widow Bascom.
   According to Rob, it happened "the day before yesterday." He was walking past her house and she asked him to help her move some flower pots. Since the Book of Shaker said to do a good turn, Rob moved the pots. The Widow gave him buttermilk and gingersnaps. He also met her hired hand, Ira Long. They complimented Rob on the way he helped Apron. The Widow invited Rob to stop in anytime.

4. How did Rob get the opportunity to go to the Rutland Fair?
   Rob had mentioned to the Widow Bascom that he would like to go. She told Mr. Tanner. He wanted a boy to help him show the twin oxen, so he asked Haven Peck if Rob could go.

5. How did Mama and Aunt Carrie feel about Rob going to Rutland?
   Mama was happy. Aunt Carrie wasn't sure, but then gave him ten cents to spend. She told him to keep the money a secret.

6. What did Rob tell Pinky about the Widow Bascom?
   He told Pinky the Widow was "some improved."

7. What one word did Papa say as Rob got out of the wagon at the Tanners' house?
   He said, "Manners."

8. List, in order, the things Rob did when he got to the fair.
   They headed or the stock area. He and Mrs. Tanner looked for a rest room. Next, they went to see Bob and Bib, and get them yoked. They took the oxen to a show area and got their pictures taken. Rob showed the oxen in the exhibition ring. He went to get Pinky and found out she had rolled in manure. He bought a used piece of saddle soap with his dime, and washed her off. He showed Pinky. While showing Pinky, he wiped his head, and the smell of the manure still on his hand made him sick. Just as the judge got to him, he threw up.

9. Did Pinky win a prize? If so, what was it?
   She won first prize and a blue ribbon for the best behaved pig.

Chapters 11-12

1. Did Rob tell his parents that he got sick at the fair?
    No, he did not.

2. How did Rob feel about going to the fair?
    It felt like he had been to a star.

3. What happened when Ira Long, Rob, and Papa tried to weasel Ira's dog, Hussy?
    Hussy killed the weasel. She was hurt so badly in the process that Papa had to shoot her. Papa said he would never again weasel a dog.

4. What problem did Papa think there might be with Pinky?
    He thought she might be barren.

5. Did Haven Peck want Rob to be just like him when he grew up?
    No, he did not. He wanted Rob to be educated, and to possibly use chemicals on the farm.

6. What did Mr. Tanner say about Mr. Peck?
    Mr. Tanner said Mr. Peck was the best butcher in the county.

7. Rob said he wanted a store-bought, red and black plaid coat. What was Papa's response?
    He said Mrs. Peck would make Rob's coat. Rob could have a store-bought coat when he could earn one. He also said Rob would be a man one day soon.

8. What did Papa tell Rob while they were sitting by the fire in the parlor?
    He told Rob it was his last winter. He knew he was sick and would die within the year. He said Rob would have to grow up and become a man, even though he was only thirteen. He would have to take care of his mother, Aunt Carrie, and the farm.

Chapters 13-15

1. Mr. Tanner asked Rob about Haven Peck's health. What was Rob's answer?
    He said his father was sturdy, and had never missed a day slaughtering in his life.

2. What did Mr. Tanner think of farming?
    He said there was not higher calling than animal husbandry and making things grow.

3. What religion were Mr. and Mrs. Tanner?
    They were Baptists.

4. How was the apple crop?
    It was bad. There were few apples.

5. What happened to Pinky, and why?
    She was barren, so Papa and Rob killed and butchered her.

6. What did Rob say he wanted to do? What did he do?
    He wanted to run and cry and scream. He stood near Pinky and helped his father.

7. Which day was the day no pigs would die? Why?
    Papa died in his sleep on May third. The neighbors were attending his funeral later that day.

8. What did Rob find in the cigar box under his father's tools?
    He found a scrap of paper and a pencil stub. His father had been practicing writing his name on the paper.

9. What did Rob do after he sent his mother and Aunt Carrie to bed with cups of hot tea?
    He went out to the orchard to be alone with his father and say goodnight to him.

MULTIPLE CHOICE STUDY/QUIZ QUESTIONS
A Day No Pigs Would Die

<u>Chapters 1-2</u>
1. Why did the narrator hate Edward Thatcher?
   A. Edward had stolen his girlfriend.
   B. Edward and the narrator were competing for the highest average in school.
   C. Edward had made fun of the narrator's clothes and Shaker ways.
   D. Edward said the narrator smelled like a pig farm.

2. How did the narrator help Apron? (List the things he did, in order.)
   A. He tied one pants leg to a tree.
   B. He tied one pants leg around the calf's head.
   C. He hit and stoned Apron until she started forward
   D. Apron started running again, and he followed her.

3. What was the second problem the narrator noticed with Apron? How did he help her?
   A. Apron could not cut the umbilical cord, so he did it with his knife.
   B. Apron could not breathe. He pulled on a hard ball in her throat.
   C. Apron could not walk. He stood next to her lame foot and encouraged her.
   D. Apron was dehydrated. He got some water from a nearby pond.

4. What was the narrator's name? What was his father's name?
   A. The narrator was Robert Peck. The father was Haven Peck.
   B. The narrator was Richard Haven. The father was Peter Haven.
   C. The narrator and the father were both named Harrison Newton.
   D. The narrator was Newton Park. The father was Ira Robert Park.

5. Who found the narrator?
   A. His father found him.
   B. Ira Long found him.
   C. The Widow Bascom found him.
   D. Benjamin Tanner found him.

6. True or False: The narrator was very bloody after the encounter with the cow.
   A. True
   B. False

7. True or False: The town doctor sewed up the narrator's torn arm.
   A. True
   B. False

A Day No Pigs Would Die Multiple Choice Study Questions Page 2

8. What was the father's occupation?
    A. He was a blacksmith.
    B. He was a pig butcher.
    C. He was a minister.
    D. He was a cattle rancher.

9. True or False: The narrator liked the smell his father had on Saturday afternoons.
    A. True
    B. False

A Day No Pigs Would Die Multiple Choice Study Questions Page 3

Chapters 3-4

1. Who was **not** in the "odd parade"?.
   A. Mr. Tanner
   B. Apron
   C. Rob
   D. two calves

2. What did Ben Tanner give Rob as a gift of thanks for delivering Apron's calf?
   A. He gave Rob one of the calves.
   B. He gave Rob a twenty dollar bill.
   C. He gave Rob a puppy.
   D. He gave Rob a piglet.

3. True or False: Haven Peck accepted the gift just for being a good neighbor.
   A. True
   B. False

4. What did Rob name his pet?
   A. He named it Pinky.
   B. He named it Samson.
   C. He named it Bib.
   D. He named it Lil' Apron.

5. Rob said he disagreed with his father about one Shaker law in particular. What was it?
   A. He disagreed with the law that said they could not sing and dance.
   B. He disagreed with the law that said they could not read fiction.
   C. He disagreed with the law that said they could only have other Shakers for friends.
   D. He disagreed with the law that said they could not go to baseball games on Sunday.

6. True or False: Haven Peck could not read or write.
   A. True
   B. False

7. What did Haven Peck say his mission was?
   A. He said his mission was spreading the Shaker beliefs.
   B. He said his mission was raising well behaved children.
   C. He said he mission was killing pigs.
   D. He said his mission was keeping his farm in order.

A Day No Pigs Would Die Multiple Choice Study Questions Page 4

8. What, according to Haven Peck, made Vermont a good state?
   A. Most of the people were Shakers.
   B. The soil was fertile and the taxes were low.
   C. Most of the people were descended from Ethan Allen and the Green Mountain Boys.
   D. The people of Vermont knew they could turn grass into milk and corn into hogs.

9. How did Rob feel the first night he had his pet?
   A. He was afraid he would not be able to take care of her.
   B. He thought he was the luckiest boy in Learning.
   C. He was disappointed because she did not want to play with him.
   D. He felt like it was Christmas morning.

A Day No Pigs Would Die Multiple Choice Study Questions Page 5

<u>Chapters 5-6</u>

1. What, according to Rob, was the best part of Shaker Meeting?
    A. Everyone danced and sang hymns.
    B. He sat where he could see Becky Tate but she could not see him.
    C. There was a luncheon after the meeting and he liked the cakes the women brought.
    D. His father let him put the money in the collection plate.

2. True or False: Ben Tanner's farm looked prosperous, compared to the Peck farm.
    A. True
    B. False

3. After whom was Rob named?
    A. He was named after Robert Newton, his mother's father.
    B. He was named after Reverend Henry Roberts, a famous Shaker minister.
    C. He was named after Robert Merrill, a Shaker who developed a new way of farming.
    D. He was named after Major Robert Roger, who had done a lot with the Indians.

4. Why did Mama call Rob to the barn?
    A. She wanted to show him the cat, Miss Sarah, and her new kittens.
    B. She wanted him to clean up a mess Pinky had made.
    C. She wanted him to help her put the tools away.
    D. She wanted to show him the new knife she bought Papa for his birthday.

5. True or False: By June, Pinky was twice as big as Rob.
    A. True
    B. False

6. What happened when Aunt Matty saw Rob's D in English?
    A. She said he should quit school and concentrate on farming.
    B. She said the schools were not as good as they used to be.
    C. She offered to tutor him.
    D. She told Mama it was her fault because she was not strict enough.

7. Aunt Matty had a reason for Rob's D in English. What was it?
    A. She said all he ever thought about was girls.
    B. She said he didn't read enough.
    C. She said the teacher did not explain things well enough.
    D. She said the D was due to his Shaker upbringing

A Day No Pigs Would Die Multiple Choice Study Questions Page 6

8. What was Aunt Matty's job before she married Uncle Hue?
   A. She was a librarian.
   B. She was an English teacher.
   C. She ran a boarding house.
   D. She was an editor for a publishing company.

9. What was the reason, according to Aunt Matty, that Rob didn't know grammar?
   A. He didn't know how to diagram sentences.
   B. He didn't know the parts of speech.
   C. He was out sick when grammar was taught.
   D. He could not read well enough to understand the sentences.

A Day No Pigs Would Die Multiple Choice Study Questions Page 7

Chapters 7-8
1. What did the hawk catch?
   A. It caught Pinky.
   B. It caught a raccoon.
   C. It caught a cottontail rabbit.
   D. It caught Rob by the arm.

2. Did Rob know the amount of food Pinky was eating?
   A. Yes, he kept a record of how much he fed Pinky.
   B. No, he relied on his mother to keep track for him.

3. What did Rob intend to do with Pinky?
   A. He wanted to show her at fairs and win a lot of money.
   B. He wanted to keep her as a pet.
   C. He wanted her to be a brood sow.
   D. He wanted to trade her for an ox.

4. What was Rob's favorite sight?
   A. It was the heavens at sundown.
   B. It was Pinky in her house.
   C. It was a chocolate cake on the dinner table.
   D. It was his father's smile.

5. True or False: Sebring Hillman had gone to the graveyard to bury his sister.
   A. True
   B. False

6. Identify the person: She was a relative of Haven Peck's. She got pregnant by Sebring Hillman. She drowned the baby, then hung herself.
   A. Louanne Long
   B. Patience Goodson
   C. Letty Phelps
   D. Hattie Barrett

A Day No Pigs Would Die Multiple Choice Study Questions Page 8

7. Identify the person: She was a relative of Haven Peck's. She got pregnant by Sebring Hillman. She drowned the baby, then hung herself.
   A. Louanne Long
   B. Patience Goodson
   C. Letty Phelps
   D. Hattie Barrett

8. What did Haven Peck do when he found Sebring Hillman? List the events in order.
   A. He drove them all home for breakfast.
   B. He agreed with Sebrin'gs decision.
   C. He helped Sebring dig in the earth and find the smaller coffin.
   D. He had his gun with him, but said it was for varmints, not neighbors.

9. True or False: Sebring wanted to bury the child in his plot.
   A. True
   B. False

A Day No Pigs Would Die Multiple Choice Study Questions Page 9

Chapters 9-10
1. What did Aunt Carrie think was shameful?
    A. Mr. Tanner kissed his wife in public.
    B. The Widow Bascom and her hired man were living together.
    C. Mrs. Long was singing while working in her garden.
    D. The Pecks' oldest daughter wore overalls while she did the planting on her farm.

2. What did the Widow Bascom do when Rob and Jacob ran through her strawberry patch?
    A. She threw a bucket of dirty water on them.
    B. She whacked both of them with a broom.
    C. She went to talk to their parents.
    D. She caught them and made them weed the garden every week all summer.

3. What did Rob do on his second run-in with the Widow Bascom?
    A. He white-washed her fence.
    B. He built a house for her pig.
    C. He brought her cows in from the field.
    D. He moved her flower pots.

4. True or False: Rob asked Mr. Tanner to take him to the Rutland Fair.
    A. True
    B. False

5. How did Mama and Aunt Carrie feel about Rob going to Rutland?
    A. Mama was happy. Aunt Carrie wasn't sure, but then gave him ten cents to spend.
    B. Neither of them thought he should go, because it was too worldly.
    C. Aunt Carrie was glad, but Mama was afraid he would get lost.
    D. They both thought it was a wonderful idea.

6. True or False: Rob told Pinky the Widow was "some improved."
    A. True
    B. False

7. What did Papa say as Rob got out of the wagon at the Tanners' house?
    A. He said, "Remember your Shaker ways."
    B. He said, "Manners."
    C. He said, "Do us proud."
    D. He said, "Much obliged, neighbor."

A Day No Pigs Would Die Multiple Choice Study Questions Page 10

8. List, in order, the things Rob did when he got to the fair.
   A. He showed Pinky.
   B. He and Mrs. Tanner looked for a rest room.
   C. Just as the judge got to him, he threw up.
   D. Rob showed the oxen in the exhibition ring.

9. Which sentence describes the outcome of the pig judging contest for Pinky?
   A. She won a gold ribbon for heaviest pig in her age group.
   B. She was disqualified because she was dirty and smelled like manure.
   C. She did not win a prize, but got a certificate of participation.
   D. She won first prize and a blue ribbon for the best behaved pig.

A Day No Pigs Would Die Multiple Choice Study Questions Page 11

Chapters 11-12

1. Did Rob tell his parents that he got sick at the fair?
    A. Yes, he did.
    B. No, he did not.

2. How did Rob feel about going to the fair?
    A. He liked the city and wanted to move there.
    B. It felt like he had been to a star.
    C. He was glad he went, but did not want to go again.
    D. He did not enjoy it at all.

3. What happened when Ira Long, Rob, and Papa tried to weasel Ira's dog, Hussy?
    A. Hussy killed the weasel, then bit Ira.
    B. The weasel got scared and ran away.
    C. Hussy refused to fight and they had to kill the weasel for her.
    D. Hussy was hurt so badly in the process that Papa had to shoot her.

4. True or False: Papa thought Pinky might be barren.
    A. True
    B. False

5. True or False: Haven Peck wanted Rob to be just like him when he grew up.
    A. True
    B. False

6. What did Mr. Tanner say about Mr. Peck?
    A. He said Mr. Peck was a good farmer but didn't have much business sense.
    B. He said Mr. Peck was a wonderful neighbor.
    C. He said Mr. Peck would be more successful if he adopted modern ways of doing things.
    D. Mr. Tanner said Mr. Peck was the best butcher in the county.

7. Rob said he wanted a store-bought, red and black plaid coat. What was Papa's response?
    A. Rob couldn't have a store-bought coat until he stopped growing.
    B. Mama's feelings would be hurt if Rob did not wear the clothes she made.
    C. Rob could have a store-bought coat when he could earn one.
    D. Rob could have the coat if he sold Pinky to get the money.

A Day No Pigs Would Die Multiple Choice Study Questions Page 12

8. What did Papa tell Rob while they were sitting by the fire in the parlor?
    A. He was going to lose the farm if he didn't pay the mortgage in thirty days.
    B. He and Mama were planning to send Rob to town to go to school.
    C. Mama was going to have another baby.
    D. He knew he was sick and would die within the year.

A Day No Pigs Would Die Multiple Choice Study Questions Page 13

Chapters 13-15

1. Mr. Tanner asked Rob about Haven Peck's health. What was Rob's answer?
   A. He said his father was sturdy, and had never missed a day slaughtering in his life.
   B. He said his father was sick and would probably die soon.
   C. He said the family did not want to talk about private information with anyone.
   D. He said his father needed a doctor but did not have the money to go to one.

2. Who said there was no higher calling than animal husbandry and making things grow?
   A. Mr. Peck
   B. Mr. Tanner
   C. Mr. Long
   D. Mama

3. True or False: Mr. and Mrs. Tanner were Shakers.
   A. True
   B. False

4. How was the apple crop?
   A. It was the best ever.
   B. It was bad. There were few apples.
   C. It was almost as good as the year before.
   D. It was late coming and the apples were very small.

5. What happened to Pinky, and why?
   A. Rob sold her to buy medicine for his father.
   B. A pack of wild dogs killed her.
   C. She got sick and died.
   D. She was barren, so Papa and Rob killed and butchered her.

6. What did Rob say he wanted to do? What did he do?
   A. He wanted to bury her in the family plot, but he butchered her instead.
   B. He wanted to run and cry and scream, but he stood near Pinky and helped his father.
   C. He wanted to go after the dogs, but he cleaned up the yard instead.
   D. He wanted to shout for joy, but he stayed quiet and calm.

A Day No Pigs Would Die Multiple Choice Study Questions Page 14

7. Which day was the day no pigs would die? Why?
    A. It was Christmas, and no work was done on that day.
    B. There was a blizzard on April first, and Papa could not get out to do his work.
    C. Papa died in his sleep on May third, and the neighbors attended his funeral.
    D. Ben Tanner's barn had burned down, and everyone helped him rebuild on March tenth.

8. What did Rob find in the cigar box under his father's tools?
    A. He found several hundred dollars his father had been saving.
    B. He found a scrap of paper with his father's name on it and a pencil stub.
    C. He found a bill from the general store that his father had not paid.
    D. He found his father's will.

9. What did Rob do after he sent his mother and Aunt Carrie to bed with cups of hot tea?
    A. He went to his room and wrote a letter to his father.
    B. He sat by the fire and read the Book of Shaker.
    C. He went out to the orchard to be alone with his father and say goodnight to him.
    D. He broke his father's best knife in anger.

STUDENT ANSWER SHEET-MULTIPLE CHOICE/QUIZ QUESTIONS

Chapters 1-2	Chapters 3-4	Chapters 5-6
1. _____	1. _____	1. _____
2. _____	2. _____	2. _____
3. _____	3. _____	3. _____
4. _____	4. _____	4. _____
5. _____	5. _____	5. _____
6. _____	6. _____	6. _____
7. _____	7. _____	7. _____
8. _____	8. _____	8. _____
9. _____	9. _____	9. _____

Chapters 7-8	Chapters 9-10	Chapters 11-12	Chapters 13-15
1. _____	1. _____	1. _____	1. _____
2. _____	2. _____	2. _____	2. _____
3. _____	3. _____	3. _____	3. _____
4. _____	4. _____	4. _____	4. _____
5. _____	5. _____	5. _____	5. _____
6. _____	6. _____	6. _____	6. _____
7. _____	7. _____	7. _____	7. _____
8. _____	8. _____	8. _____	8. _____
	9. _____		9. _____

ANSWER KEY-MULTIPLE CHOICE/QUIZ QUESTIONS
A Day No Pigs Would Die

Chapters 1-2	Chapters 3-4	Chapters 5-6
1. C	1. C	1. B
2. B, D, A, C	2. D	2. A TRUE
3. B	3. B FALSE	3. D
4. A	4. A	4. A
5. D	5. D	5. B FALSE
6. A	6. A TRUE	6. C
7. B FALSE	7. C	7. D
8. B	8. D	8. B
9. B FALSE	9. B	9. A

Chapters 7-8	Chapters 9-10	Chapters 11-12	Chapters 13-15
1. C	1. B	1. B	1. A
2. A	2. B	2. B	2. B
3. C	3. D	3. D	3. B FALSE
4. A	4. B FALSE	4. A TRUE	4. B
5. B FALSE	5. A	5. B FALSE	5. D
6. C	6. A TRUE	6. D	6. B
7. C	7. B	7. C	7. C
8. D C B A	8. B, D, A, C	8. D	8. B
9. B FALSE	9. D		9. C

PREREADING VOCABULARY WORKSHEETS

Vocabulary *A Day No Pigs Would Die*

Chapters 1-2
Part I: Using Prior Knowledge and Context Clues
Below are the sentences in which the vocabulary words appear in the text. Read the sentence. Use any clues you can find in the sentence combined with your prior knowledge, and write what you think the underlined words mean on the lines provided.

1. But instead I was up on the ridge near the old **_spar_** mine above our farm . . .
   _____

2. Picking up a stone, I threw it into some **_bracken_** ferns, hard as I could.
   _____

3. As I went down, losing my grip on the calf's neck, her hoof caught my shinbone and it really **_smarted_**.
   _____

4. All I knew was that I was snarled up in a **_passel_** of wet stuff. . .
   _____

5. "I know what that is. It's a **_goiter_**."
   _____

6. Later I woke up when Mama brought me a dish of hot **_succotash_** and a warm glass of milking, fresh from the evening pail.
   _____

7. "Anything'll bite, be it **_provoked_**."
   _____

8. He smelled just like the big brown bar of soap that he used, and sometimes there was some store-bought **_pomade_** on his hair.
   _____

Vocabulary *A Day No Pigs Would Die* Chapters 1-2 Continued

Part II: Determining the Meaning   Match the vocabulary words to their dictionary definitions.

____ 1. spar
____ 2. bracken
____ 3. smarted
____ 4. passel
____ 5. goiter
____ 6. succotash
____ 7. provoked
____ 8. pomade

A. a stew of corn, lima beans, and tomatoes
B. a large quantity or group
C. an enlargement of the thyroid gland
D. nonmetallic light-colored mineral
E. caused a stinging pain
F. incited to anger or resentment
G. a weedy fern
H. a perfumed hair ointment

Vocabulary *A Day No Pigs Would Die*

Chapters 3-4

Part I: Using Prior Knowledge and Context Clues
Below are the sentences in which the vocabulary words appear in the text. Read the sentence. Use any clues you can find in the sentence combined with your prior knowledge, and write what you think the underlined words mean on the lines provided.

1. "Now, thanks to your **_stout_** son, Haven, I got me the pair."
   ___

2. Papa's sharp nudge in my ribs with the handle of his **_mattock_** helped my being so prompt and grateful.
   ___

3. Anybody who had half an eye could see she was a pig. And what a **_brood_** sow she'd make.
   ___

4. "Haven Peck," said Mr. Tanner, "what I really come here for is to ask you to help me **_yoke_** these two demons come fall. Will you?"
   ___

5. "We're going to let Solomon use a **_capstan_**--just a great big crank."
   ___

6. "No," I said. "It's too **_blundersome_**."
   ___

7. "Papa, it sure is **_mirthful_** that somebody who knows history like Miss Malcom knows it has never heard of a great man like Abner Doubleday."
   ___

8. We can look at sundown and se it all, so that it wets the eye and **_hastens_** the heart.
   ___

9. In each hole he used a **_mallet_** to pound in a **_trunnel_** peg of white oak that he had soaking in
10. linseed oil.
    ___

Vocabulary *A Day No Pigs Would Die* Chapters 3-4 Continued

Part II: Determining the Meaning Match the vocabulary words to their dictionary definitions.

_____ 1. stout   A. a short-handled hammer with a large head
_____ 2. mattock   B. a crossbar with two U-shaped pieces
_____ 3. brood   C. full of gladness and gaiety
_____ 4. yoke   D. moves or acts swiftly
_____ 5. capstan   E. strong in body
_____ 6. blundersome   F. a wooden peg that swells when wet
_____ 7. mirthful   G. a digging tool with a flat blade
_____ 8. hastens   H. causing mistakes
_____ 9. mallet   I. used for reproduction
_____ 10. trunnel   J. an apparatus used for hoisting weights

Vocabulary *A Day No Pigs Would Die*

Chapters 5-6
Part I: Using Prior Knowledge and Context Clues
Below are the sentences in which the vocabulary words appear in the text. Read the sentence. Use any clues you can find in the sentence combined with your prior knowledge, and write what you think the underlined words mean on the lines provided.

1. Pinky watched it for a moment or two, but didn't find it near as ***comely*** as butternuts.
   _____

2. From high on the ridge, Pinky and I could look down and see Mr. Tanner's farm. It sure looked ***prosperous*** next to ours.
   _____

3. But she sure waded it fast as ***fury***.
   _____

4. If Aunt Matty wanted to play the cornet, I was ***partial*** to it.
   _____

5. She gave a big sigh (like Solomon when he's pulling the plow and comes to the end of a furrow) ad I knew that grammar sure was a ***tribulation***.
   _____

6. An angry teacher is bad aplenty, but I didn't know how good I could ***fend*** off an angry Baptist.
   _____

7. One look from that old witch, they said, would mildew ***silage*** and peel paint.
   _____

Vocabulary *A Day No Pigs Would Die* Chapters 5-6 Continued

Part II: Determining the Meaning Match the vocabulary words to their dictionary definitions.

_____ 1. comely
_____ 2. prosperous
_____ 3. fury
_____ 4. partial
_____ 5. tribulation
_____ 6. fend
_____ 7. silage

A. successful
B. to ward off
C. fermented green plants
D. violent anger; rage
E. distress; suffering
F. pleasing and wholesome in appearance
G. having a liking or fondness for

Vocabulary *A Day No Pigs Would Die*

<u>Chapters 7-8</u>
Part I: Using Prior Knowledge and Context Clues
Below are the sentences in which the vocabulary words appear in the text. Read the sentence. Use any clues you can find in the sentence combined with your prior knowledge, and write what you think the underlined words mean on the lines provided.

1. Seeing his ***talons*** were buried in its fur, the hawk was being whipped through that juniper bush for fair.
   _____

2. The tiny claws dug into my shoulder, right through my shirt, until I held her close to make her ***fret*** no more of falling.
   _____

3. I got dressed so fast my trousers were on front side back, and it felt sort of ***queer***.
   _____

4. Before I could ask what was ***astir*** or where were we going. Papa threw me up on the wagon seat and covered me with an old buffalo robe.
   _____

5. Papa held the gun in the crook of his arm, ***muzzle*** down.
   _____

6. "It's for ***varmints***," Papa said, "not for neighbors."
   _____

7. "You don't have a ***slicker***," Papa said, almost like asking.
   _____

Part II: Determining the Meaning Match the vocabulary words to their dictionary definitions.

____ 1.	talons	A.	the forward end of the barrel of a firearm
____ 2.	fret	B.	to be uneasy
____ 3.	queer	C.	one that is undesirable or troublesome
____ 4.	astir	D.	moving about
____ 5.	muzzle	E.	a raincoat made of plastic or rubber
____ 6.	varmints	F.	strange, odd
____ 7.	slicker	G.	claws of a bird of prey

Chapters 9-10
Part I: Using Prior Knowledge and Context Clues
Below are the sentences in which the vocabulary words appear in the text. Read the sentence. Use any clues you can find in the sentence combined with your prior knowledge, and write what you think the underlined words mean on the lines provided.

1. Them two living under the same roof, without benefit of ***clergy***.
   _____

2. And Mr. Tanner was as proud of that ***brace*** of grays as he was of Bob and Bib.
   _____

3. All we did was find a pair of ***shanties***, one marked LADIES and the other one GENTS.
   _____

4. "***Exhibition*** only, and not for sale."
   _____

5. Until Mr. Tanner gave me a healthy ***prod*** in the backside with his ***goad*** and said, "Git!"
6. _____

7. "I don't want to put anything on right now. I just want to take off this cussed ***corset***."
   _____

Part II: Determining the Meaning Match the words to their dictionary definitions.

____ 1. clergy   A. undergarment that supports waist and hips
____ 2. brace   B. a pair of like things
____ 3. shanties   C. a long stick with a pointed end
____ 4. exhibition   D. shacks
____ 5. prod   E. to jab or poke with a pointed object
____ 6. goad   F. people ordained for religious service
____ 7. corset   G. a public showing

Vocabulary *A Day No Pigs Would Die*

Chapters 11-12

Part I: Using Prior Knowledge and Context Clues

Below are the sentences in which the vocabulary words appear in the text. Read the sentence. Use any clues you can find in the sentence combined with your prior knowledge, and write what you think the underlined words mean on the lines provided.

1. I never let on that I got a touch of the ***vapors*** and lost all my breakfast on the judge's shoe.
   _____

2. Soon as we got there, that burlap jumped around like it was ***loco***.
   _____

3. She was a sweet little dog, and all the way home, as I was holding her, I wondered how well she's ***fare*** against a weasel.
   _____

4. Papa put a bullet in her, and her whole body jerked to a ***quivering*** stillness.
   _____

5. "We could a bred her to boar at the third. Maybe she's ***barren***."
   _____

6. "The hurt's inside her. No need to ***fester*** it."
   _____

7. As I climbed up the ridge, I started searching the trees for a gray, a big fat one with a full ***paunch***.
   _____

8. "You have your schooling. You'll read and write and ***cipher***."
   _____

Vocabulary *A Day No Pigs Would Die* Chapters 11-12 Continued

Part II: Determining the Meaning   Match the vocabulary words to their dictionary definitions.

____ 1. vapors   A. incapable of producing offspring
____ 2. loco   B. to get along
____ 3. fare   C. to solve problems in arithmetic
____ 4. quivering   D. low spirits
____ 5. barren   E. to irritate
____ 6. fester   F. rapid shaking
____ 7. paunch   G. a potbelly
____ 8. cipher   H. mad; insane

Vocabulary *A Day No Pigs Would Die*

Chapters 13-15

Part I: Using Prior Knowledge and Context Clues

Below are the sentences in which the vocabulary words appear in the text. Read the sentence. Use any clues you can find in the sentence combined with your prior knowledge, and write what you think the underlined words mean on the lines provided.

1. There's no higher calling than animal **husbandry**, and making things live and grow.
   _____

2. Moving, breathing, but down, I helped roll her over on her back, standing **astride** her and holding her two forelegs straight up in the air.
   _____

3. "No cause to **rouse** yourself. I'll do the chores."
   _____

4. His fee would not be high as he was also the County **Coroner**.
   _____

Part II: Determining the Meaning   Match the vocabulary words to their dictionary definitions.

_____ 1. husbandry   A. a public officer who investigates deaths
_____ 2. astride   B. to awaken
_____ 3. rouse   C. with a leg on each side
_____ 4. coroner   D. breeding livestock

ANSWER SHEET PREREADING VOCABULARY
A Day No Pigs Would Die

Directions: Fill in the correct chapter number. Use as many of the lines as needed.

<table>
<tr><td colspan="2" align="center"><u>Chapter</u> ____</td><td></td><td colspan="2" align="center"><u>Chapter</u> ____</td><td></td></tr>
<tr><td><u>Part 1</u></td><td></td><td><u>Pt.2</u></td><td><u>Part 1</u></td><td></td><td><u>Pt.2</u></td></tr>
<tr><td>1.</td><td>_____</td><td>___</td><td>1.</td><td>_____</td><td>___</td></tr>
<tr><td>2.</td><td>_____</td><td>___</td><td>2.</td><td>_____</td><td>___</td></tr>
<tr><td>3.</td><td>_____</td><td>___</td><td>3.</td><td>_____</td><td>___</td></tr>
<tr><td>4.</td><td>_____</td><td>___</td><td>4.</td><td>_____</td><td>___</td></tr>
<tr><td>5.</td><td>_____</td><td>___</td><td>5.</td><td>_____</td><td>___</td></tr>
<tr><td>6.</td><td>_____</td><td>___</td><td>6.</td><td>_____</td><td>___</td></tr>
<tr><td>7.</td><td>_____</td><td>___</td><td>7.</td><td>_____</td><td>___</td></tr>
<tr><td>8.</td><td>_____</td><td>___</td><td>8.</td><td>_____</td><td>___</td></tr>
<tr><td>9.</td><td>_____</td><td>___</td><td>9.</td><td>_____</td><td>___</td></tr>
<tr><td>10.</td><td>_____</td><td>___</td><td>10.</td><td>_____</td><td>___</td></tr>
</table>

<table>
<tr><td colspan="2" align="center"><u>Chapter</u> ____</td><td></td><td colspan="2" align="center"><u>Chapter</u> ____</td><td></td></tr>
<tr><td><u>Part 1</u></td><td></td><td><u>Pt.2</u></td><td><u>Part 1</u></td><td></td><td><u>Pt.2</u></td></tr>
<tr><td>1.</td><td>_____</td><td>___</td><td>1.</td><td>_____</td><td>___</td></tr>
<tr><td>2.</td><td>_____</td><td>___</td><td>2.</td><td>_____</td><td>___</td></tr>
<tr><td>3.</td><td>_____</td><td>___</td><td>3.</td><td>_____</td><td>___</td></tr>
<tr><td>4.</td><td>_____</td><td>___</td><td>4.</td><td>_____</td><td>___</td></tr>
<tr><td>5.</td><td>_____</td><td>___</td><td>5.</td><td>_____</td><td>___</td></tr>
<tr><td>6.</td><td>_____</td><td>___</td><td>6.</td><td>_____</td><td>___</td></tr>
<tr><td>7.</td><td>_____</td><td>___</td><td>7.</td><td>_____</td><td>___</td></tr>
<tr><td>8.</td><td>_____</td><td>___</td><td>8.</td><td>_____</td><td>___</td></tr>
<tr><td>9.</td><td>_____</td><td>___</td><td>9.</td><td>_____</td><td>___</td></tr>
<tr><td>10.</td><td>_____</td><td>___</td><td>10.</td><td>_____</td><td>___</td></tr>
</table>

ANSWER KEY-PREREADING VOCABULARY WORKSHEETS
A Day No Pigs Would Die

Chapters 1-2
1. D
2. G
3. E
4. B
5. C
6. A
7. F
8. H

Chapters 3-4
1. E
2. G
3. I
4. B
5. J
6. H
7. C
8. D
9. A
10. F

Chapters 5-6
1. F
2. A
3. D
4. G
5. E
6. B
7. C

Chapters 7-8
1. G
2. B
3. F
4. D
5. A
6. C
7. E

Chapters 9-10
1. F
2. B
3. D
4. G
5. E
6. C
7. A

Chapters 11-12
1. D
2. H
3. B
4. F
5. A
6. E
7. G
8. C

Chapters 13-15
1. D
2. C
3. B
4. A

DAILY LESSONS

LESSON ONE

Student Objectives
1. To preview the *A Day No Pigs Would Die* Unit
2. To receive books and other related materials (study guides, reading assignment)
3. To relate prior knowledge to the new material
4. To become familiar with the vocabulary for Chapters 1-2
5. To preview the study questions for Chapters 1-2

Activity #1
Use books, magazines, and travel brochures to introduce students to the setting of the novel, a farm in Vermont. Have students either cut out pictures or make drawings based on the pictures. Arrange the pictures on a bulletin board.

Some information about the Shaker religion and way of life is included with this lesson. You may want to supplement it with additional books. Explain that while Robert Newton Peck's family were Shakers, they did not live in an exclusively Shaker community.

Activity #2
Distribute the materials students will use in this unit. Explain in detail how students are to use these materials.

Study Guides Students should preview the study guide questions before each reading assignment to get a feeling for what events and ideas are important in that section. After reading the section, students will (as a class or individually) answer the questions to review the important events and ideas from that section of the book. Students should keep the study guides as study materials for the unit test.

Reading Assignment Sheet You need to fill in the reading assignment sheet to let students know when their reading has to be completed. You can either write the assignment sheet on a side blackboard or bulletin board and leave it there for students to see each day, or you can duplicate copies for each student to have. In either case, you should advise students to become very familiar with the reading assignments so they know what is expected of them.

Unit Outline You may find it helpful to distribute copies of the Unit Outline to your students so they can keep track of upcoming lessons and assignments. You may also want to post a copy of the Unit Outline on a bulletin board and cross off each lesson as you complete it.

Extra Activities Center The resource sections of this unit contain suggestions for a library of related books and articles in your classroom as well as crossword and word search puzzles. Make an extra activities center in your room where you will keep these materials for students to use. Bring the books and articles in from the library and keep several copies of the puzzles on hand. Explain to students that these materials are available for students to use when they finish reading assignments or other class work early.

Books Each school has its own rules and regulations regarding student use of school books. Advise students of the procedures that are normal for your school.

Notebook or Unit Folder You may want the students to keep all of their worksheets, notes, and other papers for the unit together in a binder or notebook. During the first class meeting, tell them how you want them to arrange the folder. Make divider pages for vocabulary worksheets, prereading study guide questions, review activities, notes, and tests. You may want to give a grade for accuracy in keeping the folder.

Activity #3

Do a group KWL Sheet with the students (form included.) Some students will know something about Robert Newton Peck and/or *A Day No Pigs Would Die* and will have information to share. Put this information in the K column (What I Know.) Ask students what they want to find out from reading the book and record this in the W column (What I Want to Find Out.) Keep the sheet and refer back to it after reading the book. Complete the L column (What I Learned) at that time.

Activity #4

Work through the prereading vocabulary worksheet for Chapters 1-2 with the students. Tell them they will have a sheet like this to complete before reading each section of the book.

Activity #5

Show students how to preview the study questions for Chapters 1-2. Encourage students to predict what they think answers might be, to write down their predictions, and to compare these with their answers after reading the chapters.

THE SHAKERS

The official title for the Shakers is the United Society of Believers in Christ's Second Appearing. The original Shakers were Quakers who broke away from that group in 18th century England. They came to be called Shakers because of their very active religious services. Members would shake, dance, whirl, and sing in tongues.

Mother Ann Lee founded the Shaker movement in England in 1747. She was an illiterate textile worker who believed she was the second incarnation of Christ. In 1774 she came to New York, along with eight followers. In 1776 they established a community at Watervleit, New York. Mother Ann died in 1784. After that, Joseph Meacham and Lucy Wright led the movement and established 18 Shaker communities in 8 states. By 1826 the movement had 6,000 followers. The membership gradually declined, and today the Shakers are almost extinct.

The Shakers lived in communities and shared work and property. They practiced celibacy. They also believed in pacifism, free will, and equality for both sexes. The Shakers kept themselves segregated from the outside, which they called "the people of the world." They did, however, grow foods and make clothes and furniture which they sold to outsiders. The beauty and quality of their furniture was recognized all over the world.

Shakers invented many useful items, including the clothespin, a screw propeller, a turbine waterwheel, a flat broom, a circular saw, a water-powered washing machine, and a threshing machine. One invention, a vacuum pan evaporator the Shakers used to dry herbs, was also used by Gail Borden, the inventor of evaporated milk. The Shakers were the first to package and sell flower and vegetable seeds. Beautiful, hand-crafted Shaker furniture was in high demand. The Shakers experimented with methods of canning and preserving foods. The first canning factories in America used Shaker ideas.

The Shakers believed in eating a simple, healthy diet. One special Shaker treat was lemonade. The cooks soaked the lemon rind in boiling water to extract the lemon oil. They then added this lemon water to the lemon juice and sugar. Bread made with wheat germ was a part of every meal. Jams and applesauce were also present in abundance. The Shaker women made candy to sell to the world.

Shaker children enjoyed arts and crafts. Items such as their valentines, May baskets, holiday place cards, and woven Christmas ornaments may now be found in museums. The children also played games with jacks and marbles.

In 1890 a Shaker woman named Eldress Dorothy Durgin, of the Canterbury Shakers, made a hooded cloak. The cloak was beautiful, and became very popular. The women began selling the cloaks to the world, and Mrs. Grover Cleveland, wife of President Cleveland, bought one.

Museums

Canterbury Shaker Village
288 Shaker Road
Canterbury, New Hampshire 03224
603-783-9511

Hancock Shaker Village
P.O. Box 898
Pittsfield, Massachusetts 01202
413-443-0188

North Union/The Shaker Historical Society
16740 South Park Boulevard
Shaker Heights, Ohio 44120
216-921-1201

Shakertown at Pleasant Hill
3500 Lexington Road
Harrodsburg, Kentucky 40330
606-734-5411

Bibliography

Faber, Doris. *The Perfect Life: The Shakers in America*. NY. Farrar, Strauss and Giroux, 1974.
Murray, Stuart. *Shaker Heritage Guidebook*. NY, Golden Hill Press, 1994.
Thorne-Thomsen, Kathleen. *Shaker Children and Crafts*. Chicago Review Press, 1996.
Van Kolken, Diana. *Introducing the Shakers*. Ohio, Gabriel's Horn Publishing Co., 1985.

KWL
A Day No Pigs Would Die

Directions: Before reading, think about what you already know about Robert Newton Peck and/or *A Day No Pigs Would Die*. Write the information in the K column. Think about what you would like to find out from reading the book. Write your questions in the W column. After you have read the book, use the L column to write the answers to your questions from the W column, and anything else you remember from the book.

K What I Know	W What I Want to Find Out	L What I Learned

LESSON TWO

Student Objectives:
1. To read Chapters 1-2
2. To begin a sketchbook-writing journal

Activity #1

Remind students to think about the study guide questions as they listen. Begin reading the first few pages aloud to the students. Then ask for volunteers to read the remainder of Chapter 1 and Chapter 2 aloud to the class. Use an unabridged audio tape version of the novel if it is available.

Activity #2

Tell students they will be keeping a sketchbook-journal as Writing Assignment #1. Explain that a sketchbook-journal is a combination of sketches about and written responses to the story. They will be required to make an entry for each chapter in the novel.

Students can sketch memorable scenes from the chapters, or paste in magazine pictures that remind them of the events in the chapter.

The written entries should focus on each student's response to the literature, and should not merely be a plot summary. They should include comments about their thoughts and feelings while reading, any questions they have, and predictions for the next chapter.

It is up to the individual teacher to decide how to grade or respond to the journals, and whether to have students share them with the class or keep them private.

Activity #3

If time permits, allow students to begin answering the study guide questions. Tell them the answers will be due at the next class meeting.

WRITING ASSIGNMENT #1 *A Day No Pigs Would Die*
Journal Writing to Express a Personal Opinion

PROMPT

For this unit, you will keep a sketchbook-journal. This is a combination of sketches about and written responses to a story. You will make an entry for each chapter in the novel.

First, decide on the format for your sketchbook-journal. Spend some time decorating your cover and setting up the book. Make sure to include the title of each chapter and the page numbers in your copy of the book. Also date each entry.

You can sketch memorable scenes from the chapters, paste in magazine pictures, or use computer clip art. Even if you do not consider yourself a good artist, try to make some sketches. Use colors that remind you of the mood of the story. You may want to take photographs and put them in the sketchbook-journal.

The written entries should focus on your response to the literature, and should not merely be chapter summaries. They should include comments about your thoughts and feelings while reading, any questions you have, and predictions about the next chapter. Try to write at least one page for each entry. You, your class mates and your teacher will decide whether to share the journals or keep them private.

Here are some suggestions for the types of entries you may want to make.

Check Your Understanding	Explain how the story is making sense to you. Give examples and note page numbers. Establish the setting, mood, point of view, and character relationships. Discuss the stated themes.
Make Inferences	Explain your thoughts about the feelings and motives of the characters. Discuss the implied themes.
Make and Revise Predictions	At the end of each chapter, make a prediction about what you think will happen next. After you read, go back and check your predictions. Tell if you had to revise them, and why.
Ask Questions	Ask questions about scenes or events that are confusing. Record the answers if you discuss the questions in class, or later find the answer in the novel.

Give Your Opinion	Give your opinion about the literary quality of the work. Discuss the author's style, use of language, and use of literary devices. Tell why you do nor do not like the story. Tell how you feel while reading the chapters. Compare the book with others you have read.
Make Connections	Think about ways the characters and events relate to your own life and experiences. Put yourself in the character's place and discuss how you would think or feel in that situation. Try this from the point of view of the main character and a few of the minor ones.
Make Recommendations	Tell what you think the characters should do or say. Tell how you would end the story, or what you think might happen next.

LESSON THREE

Student Objectives:
1. To review the main ideas and events in Chapters 1-2
2. To identify examples of figurative language in the novel

Activity #1

Discuss the answers to the Study Guide questions for Chapters 1-2 in detail. Write the answers on the board or overhead projector so students can have the correct answers for study purposes. Encourage students to take notes. If the students own their books, encourage them to use high lighter pens to mark important passages and the answers to the study guide questions.

Note: It is a good practice in public speaking and leadership skills for individual students to take charge of leading the discussion of the study questions. Perhaps a different student could go to the front of the class and lead the discussion each day that the study questions are discussed during this unit. Of course, the teacher should guide the discussion when appropriate and be sure to fill in any gaps the students leave.

Activity #1 Minilesson: Figures of Speech

Figures of speech are literary devices that give the writer a non-literal way to describe images and events. Use the following chart to give examples of the different figures of speech. Then write "I look like a baby-faced kid" on the board. (Bryon uses this description of himself on page 1 of *That Was Then, This Is Now*.) Ask students to identify the type of figure of speech (simile.) Talk about the literal meaning. Distribute the Figure of Speech worksheet and have students work in small groups to find examples in the novel. If you want the students to continue recording examples in the remaining chapters, assign a due date for the worksheet.

COLLOQUIALISM	Conversational speech, or a manner of speaking that is related to a certain group of people or geographic area. For example, *take a shine to* means likes.
HYPERBOLE	Extreme exaggeration used to describe a person or thing. For example: *She had as many pairs of shoes as there are stars in the sky.*
IRONY	The use of words to express something different from and often opposite to their literal meaning. *Yeah, being a kid is loads of fun.*
METAPHOR	A comparison without the words like or as. *The cat is a bag of bones.*

METONYMY	A figure of speech in which one word or phrase is substituted for another with which it is closely associated, as in the use of *Washington* for the United States government or of *the sword* for military power.
ONOMATOPOEIA	The use of words such as *buzz* or *splash* that imitate the sounds associated with the objects or actions they refer to.
PARADOX	A seemingly self-contradictory statement that has some truth to it.
PERSONIFICATION	Attributing human characteristics to inanimate objects, animals, or ideas, as in *the wind howled*.
SIMILE	A comparison using the words like or as. *as pretty as pie*

FIGURES OF SPEECH

Figures of speech are literary devices that give the writer a non-literal way to describe images and events. The main types of figures of speech are hyperbole, irony, metaphor, metonymy, onomatopoeia, paradox, personification, and simile. Use the following chart to record examples of figures of speech used in *A Day No Pigs Would Die*. A sample has been done for you. Note: You may not find an example of each figure of speech in the novel.

Figure of Speech	Example from Novel, page #	Literal Meaning
simile	make him bleed like a stuck pig	he would bleed a lot

LESSON FOUR

Student Objectives
 1. To become familiar with the vocabulary for Chapters 3-4
 2. To preview the study questions for Chapters 3-4
 3. To practice correct intonation and expression in oral reading
 4. To read Chapters 3-4 orally for evaluation

Activity #1
 Tell students their oral reading ability will be evaluated. Show them copies of the Oral Reading Evaluation Form and discuss it. Model correct intonation and expression by reading the first few paragraphs of Chapter 3 aloud.

Activity #2
 Call on individual students to read a few paragraphs aloud. Encourage the other students to follow along silently in their books. If you have a student who is unwilling or unable to read in front of the group make arrangements to do his or her evaluation privately at another time.

LESSON FIVE

Student Objectives:
 1. To discuss the main ideas and events in Chapters 3-4
 2. To become familiar with the vocabulary for Chapters 5-6
 3. To preview the study questions for Chapters 5-6
 4. To read Chapters 5-6

Activity #1
 Have students work in small groups to discuss the answers to the study guide questions. Then ask a member of each group to summarize one answer for the class.

Activity #2
 Give students ten or fifteen minutes to complete the prereading vocabulary worksheet and read over the study guide questions.

Activity #3
 Give students the rest of the class period to read Chapters 5-6 silently. Tell them to finish the reading and answer the study guide questions before the next class meeting.

ORAL READING EVALUATION
A Day No Pigs Would Die

Name_____ Class_____ Date_____

SKILL	EXCELLENT	GOOD	AVERAGE	FAIR	POOR
FLUENCY	5	4	3	2	1
CLARITY	5	4	3	2	1
AUDIBILITY	5	4	3	2	1
PRONUNCIATION	5	4	3	2	1
_____	5	4	3	2	1
_____	5	4	3	2	1

TOTAL _____

GRADE _____

COMMENTS:

LESSON SIX

Student Objectives
    1. To analyze the autobiographical form of the novel
    2. To write an autobiography

Activity #1
    Write the word ***autobiography*** on the board and ask students to give the meaning. Explain the Greek origin of the root words ***auto***, meaning "same, self', ***bio*** , meaning "life', and ***graph***, meaning 'to write'.

Activity #2
    Tell students they will write an autobiography. Assign a due date, probably a few days before the writing conferences, which are scheduled for Lesson Thirteen. Distribute copies of Writing Assignment #2 and go over it in detail with students. Give them the rest of the period to work on the assignment.

Activity #3
    Distribute copies of the Writing Evaluation Form (included with this Unit Plan.) Explain to students that during Lesson Ten you will be holding individual writing conferences about this writing assignment. Make sure students are familiar with the criteria on the Writing Evaluation Form.

Follow Up: After you have graded the assignments, have a writing conference with each student. This Unit Plan schedules one in Lesson 10. After the writing conference, allow students to revise their papers using your suggestions to complete the revisions. Grade the revisions on an A-C-E scale: A = all revisions well done; C = some revisions made; E = few or no revisions made. This will speed your grading time and still give some credit for the students' efforts.

WRITING ASSIGNMENT #2 *A Day No Pigs Would Die*
Writing to Inform

PROMPT
A Day No Pigs Would Die is an autobiography. It is the story of approximately a year in the life of Robert Newton Peck as he remembers it. He includes character descriptions of the important people in his life, vivid descriptions of his family's farm and nearby towns, and details about the events that occurred. Most importantly, he offers an insight into his own reactions, thoughts, and feelings.

Your assignment is to write an autobiography.

PREWRITING
Robert Newton Peck covered about one year in his autobiography. Yours does not have to be this comprehensive. You may want to focus on one particularly interesting event or on the events of an entire year. It may help you to make a timeline of the significant events in your life. Then you can choose what you want to write about.

You may want to interview people who knew you as a young child. You should prepare a list of questions ahead of time for them to answer, and also be ready to listen to them reminisce. Tape record the interviews so that you can listen to them again as you are writing.

Organize the events in a chronological order so that the reader can follow the events as they occurred in your life.

You may want to reread Chapters 1 and 2 of *A Day No Pigs Would Die* to see how Mr. Peck introduced himself and his family to the reader.

DRAFTING
First, write a paragraph in which you introduce an important event in your life. Make sure you include background information about the setting (year, location) and the other people involved.

In the body of your autobiography, continue telling about the event or events, adding details about the other people involved. Make sure to include observations about your own thoughts and feelings.

Finally, write a concluding paragraph in which you talk abut the ways that the event/events you wrote about have influenced your life today.

PEER CONFERENCING/EDITING
When you finish the rough draft of your paper, ask another student to read it. After reading your rough draft, he/she should tell you what he/she liked best about your work, which parts were difficult to understand, and ways in which your work could be improved. Reread your paper considering your critic's comments, and make the corrections you think are necessary.

PROOFREADING
Do a final proofreading of your paper, double-checking your grammar, spelling, organization, and the clarity of your ideas.

WRITING EVALUATION FORM
A Day No Pigs Would Die

Name _____ Date _____ Class _____

Writing Assignment # _____

Circle One For Each Item:

Composition	excellent	good	fair	poor
Style	excellent	good	fair	poor
Grammar	excellent	good	fair	poor (errors noted)
Spelling	excellent	good	fair	poor (errors noted)
Punctuation	excellent	good	fair	poor (errors noted)
Legibility	excellent	good	fair	poor (errors noted)

Strengths:

Weaknesses:

Comments/Suggestions:

LESSON SEVEN

Student Objectives
1. To discuss the main ideas and events in Chapters 5-6
2. To become familiar with the vocabulary for Chapters 7-8
3. To preview the study questions for Chapters 7-8
4. To read Chapters 7-8

Activity # 1

Give each student four 1"x2" strips of colored paper or index cards--one blue, one yellow, one green, one pink. Have them put a large letter A on the blue paper, B on the yellow, C on the green, and D on the pink. Distribute copies of the Multiple Choice/Quiz questions for Chapters 5-6. Ask students to read the first question and hold up the colored paper for the correct answer. Then have them mark the correct answer on their worksheets.

Activity #2

Give students ten or fifteen minutes to do the prereading vocabulary worksheet for Chapters 7-8.

Activity #3

Put the prereading questions for Chapters 7-8 on the board or on an overhead transparency. Ask students to choose one question they would like to answer after reading. Group the students according to their choices. Have each group prepare the answer to their question after they have read the text. They may give the answer by reading the information from the text, summarizing it, or dramatizing the event.

Activity #4

Allow students to take turns reading aloud quietly to the other members of their group. Remind them that any work not finished in class must be completed before the next class meeting.

Activity #5

Tell students there will be a quiz on Chapters 1-8 during the next class meeting.

LESSON EIGHT

Student Objective
1. To discuss the main ideas and events in Chapters 7-8
2. To demonstrate understanding of the main ideas and events in Chapters 1-8
2. To become familiar with the nonfiction assignment

Activity #1
Arrange students in eight groups and assign each a study question. Give students about five minutes to prepare a short (1-2 minute) skit to answer the question. Have each group perform their skit.

Activity #2
Before class, use some of the multiple choice questions from Chapters 1-8 to create a quiz. Distribute copies of the quiz. Give students ten or fifteen minutes to complete it.

Activity #3
Distribute copies of the nonfiction assignment sheet. Explain to students that they each are to read at least one nonfiction piece. This could be a book, a magazine article, or information from an encyclopedia or the Internet. Students will fill out a nonfiction assignment sheet after completing the reading to help you (the teacher) evaluate their reading experiences and to help the students think about and evaluate their own reading experiences. Give them the due date for the assignment, Lesson Twenty.

Encourage students to read about topics that are related to the theme of the novel. Some suggestions are: the life of the Shakers, farming in Vermont, animal husbandry, state fairs, farm life in the United States from 1910 to 1940, the history of baseball, the life of Abner Doubleday, the historical significance of Ethan Allen and the Green Mountain Boys, the use of standard English versus dialect in the classroom, and voting regulations.

LESSON NINE

Student Objectives
1. To become familiar with the vocabulary for Chapters 9-10
2. To preview the study questions for Chapters 9-10
3. To read Chapters 9-10
4. To record information on a story map

Activity #1
Give students ten or fifteen minutes to complete the prereading vocabulary worksheet and go over the study guide questions.

Activity #2 Minilesson: Story Map
Distribute copies of the Story Map. Tell students the story map includes all of the elements of a story: characters, setting, problem or conflict, events, and solution or resolution. Help students fill in as many details as possible on the story map. Encourage them to reread the text to find details for the map. Tell them the completed story map will be due during Lesson Fourteen.

Alternate Activity
Instead of using the Story Map to cover the entire story, assign small groups of students to complete a map for each of the reading assignment sections. Then have each group present their information in order according to the story chapters. This will serve as a good review of the main ideas and events in the novel.

Activity #3
Give students the rest of the class period to read Chapters 9-10 silently. Remind them to complete the reading and answer the study guide questions before the next class meeting.

NONFICTION ASSIGNMENT SHEET
A Day No Pigs Would Die
(To be completed after reading the required nonfiction article)

Name _____ Date _____ Class _____

Title of Nonfiction Read _____

Written By _____ Publication Date _____

I. Factual Summary: Write a short summary of the piece you read.

II. Vocabulary:
    1. Which vocabulary words were difficult?

    2. What did you do to help yourself understand the words?

III. Interpretation: What was the main point the author wanted you to get from reading his/her work?

IV. Criticism:
    1. Which points of the piece did you agree with or find easy to believe? Why?

    2. With which points of the piece did you disagree or find difficult to believe? Why?

V. Personal Response:
    1. What do you think about this piece?

    2. How does this piece help you better understand the novel *A Day No Pigs Would Die*

STORY MAP
A Day No Pigs Would Die

CHARACTERS
Main

Minor

SETTING
Time

Place

THEME

POINT OF VIEW

PROBLEM

EVENTS

SOLUTION

LESSON TEN

Student Objectives
1. To discuss the main ideas and events in Chapters 9-10
1. To become familiar with the vocabulary for Chapters 11-12
2. To preview the study questions for Chapters 11-12
3. To read Chapters 11-12 aloud to practice reading dialog

Activity #1
Divide students into nine groups. Assign a study question to each group. Have the group draw a picture to illustrate the answer to the question, then present the picture and answer to the class.

Activity #2
Give students ten or fifteen minutes to complete the prereading vocabulary worksheet and go over the study guide questions.

Activity #3
Ask for volunteers to take the parts of the characters in the chapters. You will need a narrator, a separate speaker for the narrator's remarks, Mr. Tanner, Mrs. Tanner, Papa, Mama, and Ira Long. Have the readers sit or stand in the front of the room and read the chapters aloud. If you choose to assign the parts ahead of time, suggest that students bring simple costumes and props. They can also practice their parts at home the night before class.

LESSON ELEVEN

Student Objectives
1. To discuss the main ideas and events in Chapters 11-12
1. To become familiar with the vocabulary for Chapters 13-15
2. To preview the study questions for Chapters 13-15
3. To read Chapters 13-15

Activity #1
Review the answers to the study guide questions.

Activity #2
Give students ten or fifteen minutes to complete the prereading vocabulary worksheets and go over the study guide questions.

Activity #3
Give students the rest of the class period to read the chapters and answer the study guide questions.

LESSON TWELVE

Student Objectives
1. To discuss the main ideas and events in Chapters 13-15
2. To complete a character sketch of a main character

Activity #1
Go over the answers to the study guide questions.

Activity #2 Minilesson: Character Development
Explain that an author creates a character by giving him/her traits such as physical attributes, thoughts, and feelings. The author develops these traits by telling what the character says, does, and thinks. Writers usually base their characters at least in part on a real person or persons, and then elaborate. A good writer will make the characters believable for the readers. Since *A Day No Pigs Would Die* is autobiographical, the main character is also the author. Peck gives the reader insight into his own life.

Explain that this is a "coming-of-age" story, or bildungsroman, where the central character becomes more aware of himself because of events that occur. In this novel, the awareness comes because of Rob's experiences of killing his pet pig and having his father die.

Have students reread to look for Rob's character traits. Work with them to complete the character sketch. You may want them to complete a second sketch on one of the other characters. Remind them that there may not be as much information about the minor characters, so they should choose the character who is best described.

LESSON THIRTEEN

Student Objectives
1. To participate in an individual writing conference with the teacher
2. To work independently on other assignments

Activity #1
Choose a quiet place in the classroom to hold the conferences.

Activity #2
Give students an independent assignment to complete while you are holding the conferences. You may want to give them copies of the extra discussions scheduled for Lesson Fourteen, or have them start working on the projects scheduled for Lesson Fifteen.

LESSON FOURTEEN

Student Objective
> To discuss *A Day No Pigs Would Die* at the interpretive and critical levels

Activity #1
> Choose the questions from the Extra Writing Assignments/Discussion Questions which seem most appropriate for your students. A class discussion of these questions is most effective if students have been given the opportunity to formulate answers to the questions prior to the discussion. To this end, you may either have all the students formulate answers to all the questions, divide the class into groups and assign one or more questions to each group, or you could assign one question to each student in your class. The option you choose will make a difference in the amount of class time needed for this activity.

Activity #2
> After students have had ample time to formulate answers to the questions, begin your class discussion of the questions and the ideas presented by the questions. Be sure students take notes during the discussion so they have information to study for the unit test.

CHARACTER TRAITS CHART
Day No Pigs Would Die

CHARACTER _____

Trait_____	Trait _____	Trait _____	Trait _____
Events That Show It	Events That Show It	Events That Show It	Events That Show It

EXTRA WRITING ASSIGNMENT/DISCUSSION QUESTIONS
A Day No Pigs Would Die

<u>Interpretation</u>

1. From what point of view is the story written? How does this affect our understanding of the story?

2. What are the main conflicts in the story? Are they resolved? If so, how? If not, why not?

3. What is the setting? How important is the setting to the story? Why?

4. Why was killing Pinky so disturbing to Rob?

5. Why was Rob so excited about going to the Rutland Fair?

6. Which seemed harder for Rob to deal with; the death of his father or taking over as the man of the house?

7. Why do you think Rob reacted the way he did when his father told him he would probably die soon?

8. How did Haven Peck's religious beliefs influence his life?

9. When Miss Malcom handed back the test papers, she was laughing at something on Rob's paper. What was it? Why was she laughing at it? How did Rob feel about her laughter?

10. What were some of the conflicts between Haven Peck and his son? Which was the most serious?

11. Compare and contrast one of the characters in this book with a character in another book.

12. Discuss Mama's role in the story. Why doesn't Peck tell the readers her first name? Do you think she had much influence over him?

13. How did Haven Peck feel about not being able to vote?

14. What did Rob learn about religion in Chapter 13?

Extra Discussion Questions *A Day No Pigs Would Die* Page 2

Critical

15. Is the story believable? Why or why not?

16. How did Rob change over the course of the novel? Were these changes for the better?

17. Were the characters believable? Why or why not?

18. The author often used vivid language to describe a scene or event. Give an example of his use of vivid language that you found most effective. Tell why it was effective.

19. What was the overall mood of the story? Give examples to support your answer.

20. Identify a few of the examples of colloquialisms and discuss their contribution to the novel.

21. How does the author create suspense?

22. What problem or conflict does the author use to get the story started? How effective is it?

23. Could any of the main events be left out? Which ones? Why or why not?

24. How would the story change if there were a different narrator?

25. Which character do you know the most about? Which character do you know the least about?

26. Peck describes his confusion about Ethan Allen, The Green Mountain Boys, and Abner Doubleday. What caused his confusion?

27. There are several humorous scenes in the book. Summarize one of them. Discuss how the author made the event humorous.

28. Were you able to predict the ending? What clues did the author give?

29. Discuss the author's use of language. Is it natural? Do people you know talk the way the characters did?

30. Does the mood of the story change? How does the author show this?

Extra Discussion Questions *A Day No Pigs Would Die* Page 3

31. What words does the author use to create the atmosphere of the book?

32. Which chapter was most important? Why?

33. Were the descriptions in the book effective? Give some examples.

34. Which senses did the descriptions cause you to use? Give examples of the descriptions using hearing, seeing, touching, smelling, taste.

Personal Response
35. Did you enjoy reading *A Day No Pigs Would Die?* Why or why not?

36. Is *A Day No Pigs Would Die a* good title for the book? Why or why not? If not, what title would you suggest?

37. Did you have strong feelings while reading this book? If so, what did the author do to cause those feelings? If not, why not?

38. Will you read more of Robert Newton Peck's books? Why or why not?

39. Did Rob's experiences change the way you look at yourself? How?

40. Have you read any other stories similar to *A Day No Pigs Would Die?* If so, tell about them.

41. Would you recommend this book to another student? Why or why not?

42. What makes Robert Newton Peck a unique and different author?

43. What questions would you like to ask the author?

44. What was the funniest part of the story? What was the saddest part? What was the most exciting part?

QUOTATIONS *A Day No Pigs Would Die*

Discuss the significance of the following quotations.

1. "I don't cotton to raise a fool."

2. "The poor lamb."

3. "And he wants a fence to divide his and mine, same as I do. He knows this. A fence sets men together, not apart."

4. "Bob and Bib," said Mr. Tanner. "And the Bob of it is after you, Robert."

5. "Do you think the Lord will forgive us?"
   "I think so. Somehow, the Good Lord don't want to see no man start a cold morning with just black coffee."

6. "No, I cannot read. But our Law has been red to me. And because I could not read, I knew to listen with a full heart. It might be the last and only time I'd learn its meaning."

7. "Thanks be praised the only history I need's in our Family Bible tucked away under the bed in the Bible Box. And in the Book of Shaker."

8. "Course you haven't. Trouble with teachers today is, they don't diagram. All they think of is the Bunny Hug."

9. "Next time," said Aunt Matty, "I'll teach the pig."

10. "Rob, you feed that pig better than you feed yourself."

11. "Papa," I said, "of all the things in the world to see, I reckon the heavens at sundown has got to be my favorite sight. How about you?"

12. "She don't have folks. They left town after she drown this child, then hung herself. I can't undo what's already been did. But the little girl is mine. You hear me, Haven? This child is mine, and I claim it soul and dust."

13. "Let's go home, May."

14. "And if Iris Bascom and her man giggle in the dark, they can have my blessing for whatever it's worth."

15. "I'm always hungry," I said, "because I got a tapeworm."

16. ""Never miss a chance," Papa had said once, "to keep your mouth shut."

17. "I swear," said Papa, "I swear by the Book of Shaker and all that's holy, I will never again weasel a dog. Even if I lose every chicken I own."

18. "Hussy," I said, "you got more spunk in you than a lot of us menfolk got brains."

19. "Dying is dirty business. Like getting born."

20. "You'll do right next spring, Rob. Just take time with things. One chore done good beats two done ragged."

21. "She said I smelled of honest work, and that there was no sorry to be said or heard."

22. "I'm sure glad to be famed for something."

23. "So do I. But one thing to learn, Rob, is this. Need is a weak word. Has nothing to do with what people get. Ain't what you need that matters. It's what you do. And your mother'll do you a coat."

24. "It can't be no longer your mother and Carrie taking care of you. Soon you got to care for them. They're old, too. Years of work done that."

25. "Your father," he asked. "How's his health?"

26. "Good. Twelve's a boy, thirteen's a man."

27. "Papa works all the time. He don't never rest. And worse than that, he works inside himself. I can see it on his face. Like he's been trying all his life to catch up to something. But whatever it is, it's always ahead of him, and he can't reach it."

28. "Oh, Papa. My heart's broke."
    "So is mine," said Papa. "But I'm thankful you're a man."

29. "Robert, my name is Benjamin Franklin Tanner. All my neighbors call me Ben. I think two men who are good friends ought to front name one another."
    "And I'm Bess," his wife said, "from here on."

30. "Good night, Papa," I said. "We had thirteen good years."

LESSON FIFTEEN

Student Objectives
1. To extend the story by means of a project
2. To work cooperatively in a group

Activity #1
Allow students to choose one of the following projects. Give them the class period to complete it. If students need more time, you can assign the project as homework or add another day onto the unit plan.

PROJECT IDEAS

1. Draw a book jacket that summarizes the story.

2. Write a critique of the book.

3. Make a time line showing the important events from the story.

4. Make a diorama showing one of the scenes from the book.

5. Find the names for groups of animals, such as a brace of horses in Chapter 10. Draw pictures of the groups and write the names under the pictures.

6. Make puppets and write a puppet show to illustrate one scene from the story.

7. Write a radio or television commercial to advertise the book.

8. Design a poster to advertise the book.

9. Write a different ending to the story.

10. Make a comic book version of the story to share with younger readers.

11. Make a mobile showing the main character, secondary characters and setting.

13. Create a poster describing a scene, a character, or one of the main themes.

14. Design a tombstone for Haven Peck and write an epitaph.

15. Make a collage or mobile based on scenes from the book.

16. Diagram several sentences from the book. Put the diagrams on a poster.

17. Make and decorate a seed packet like the ones the Shakers designed and sold.

18. Find a Shaker cookbook. Make one of the recipes to share with the class.

LESSON SIXTEEN

Student Objective
    To practice writing to persuade

Activity #1
    Engage students in a discussion about pets. Ask how many have pets, and if it was easy or difficult to persuade their parents to get the pet. Ask students who do not have pets if they have asked for one. Invite pairs or small groups to perform impromptu skits persuading a parent to let them have a pet. Tell students they will write a persuasive letter to an adult, asking for a pet, or for permission to keep a pet that someone else wants removed.

Optional Topics
    Feel free to vary the topic for this writing assignment. You may want to let students choose the issue they want to write about. They may feel more strongly about an issue such as a school dress code or curfews.

Activity #2
    Distribute copies of Writing Assignment #3. Give students the rest of the period to work on the assignment.

WRITING ASSIGNMENT #3 *A Day No Pigs Would Die*
Writing to Persuade

PROMPT
Rob's father was not easily convinced to allow him to keep the pig as a pet. Then, when the pig was barren, Rob was forced to kill his pet. You will write a persuasive letter to an adult. It could be a parent or guardian, or the landlord of your apartment house. Either ask for a pet, or ask to keep a pet that you are no longer permitted to have. You may take a humorous slant, and make up a pet or write about an unusual pet.

PREWRITING
Make a list of the reasons you want your pet. Think of statements to support each of your reasons, and list them under each reason. Then number the reasons in order from most to least important.

DRAFTING
Make an introductory statement in which you describe your pet, and state your desire to have or keep it. Use one paragraph for each of your reasons. Use the supporting statements for each reason. Summarize your request and respectfully ask for a reply from the adult by a certain date, possibly a week after receiving the letter.

PEER CONFERENCING/REVISING
When you finish the rough draft, ask another student to look at it. You may want to give the student your checklist so he/she can double check for you and see that you have included all of the information. After reading, he or she should tell you what he/she liked best about your persuasive letter, which parts were difficult to understand or needed more information, and ways in which your work could be improved. Reread your persuasive letter considering your critic's comments and make the corrections you think are necessary.

PROOFREADING/EDITING
Do a final proofreading of your persuasive letter, double-checking your grammar, spelling, organization, and the clarity of your ideas.

FINAL DRAFT
Follow your teacher's guidelines for completing the final draft of your paper.

LESSON SEVENTEEN

<u>Student Objective</u>
To review all of the vocabulary work done in this unit

VOCABULARY REVIEW ACTIVITIES

1. Divide your class into two teams and have an old-fashioned spelling or definition bee.

2. Give individuals or groups of students a Vocabulary Word Search Puzzle. The person (group) to find all of the vocabulary words in the puzzle first wins.

3. Give students a Vocabulary Word Search Puzzle without the word list. The person or group to find the most vocabulary words in the puzzle wins.

4. Put a Vocabulary Crossword Puzzle onto a transparency on the overhead projector and do the puzzle together as a class.

5. Give students a Vocabulary Matching Worksheet to do.

6. Use words from the word jumble page and have students spell them correctly.

7. Have students write a story in which they correctly use as many vocabulary words as possible. Have students read their compositions orally. Post the most original compositions on your bulletin board.

8. Have students work in teams and play charades with the vocabulary words.

9. Select a word of the day and encourage students to use it correctly in their writing and speaking vocabulary.

10. Have a contest to see which students can find the most vocabulary words used in other sources. You may want to have a bulletin board available so the students can write down their word, the sentence it was used in, and the source.

11. Assign a word to each student, or let them choose a word. Have them look up the origin of the word, the part of speech, definition, a synonym, and an antonym. Then have them write a sentence using the word. Have students present their information orally to the class, or have them design a word map on paper and display the papers.

LESSON EIGHTEEN

Objective
　　　To review the main ideas presented in *A Day No Pigs Would Die*

Activity #1
　　　Choose one of the review games/activities included in the packet and spend your class period as outlined there.

Activity #2
　　　Remind students of the date for the Unit Test. Stress the review of the Study Guides and their class notes as a last minute, brush-up review for homework.

REVIEW GAMES / ACTIVITIES

1. Ask the class to make up a unit test for *A Day No Pigs Would Die*. The test should have 4 sections: multiple choice, true/false, short answer and essay. Students may use 1/2 period to make the test, including a separate answer sheet, and then swap papers and use the other 1/2 class period to take a test a classmate has devised. (open book)

2. Take 1/2 period for students to make up true and false questions (including the answers). Collect the papers and divide the class into two teams. Draw a big tic-tac-toe board on the chalk board. Make one team X and one team O. Ask questions to each side, giving each student one turn. If the question is answered correctly, that student's team's letter (X or O) is placed in the box. If the answer is incorrect, no mark is placed in the box. The object is to get three marks in a row like tic-tac-toe. You may want to keep track of the number of games won for each team.

3. Take 1/2 period for students to make up questions (true/false and short answer). Collect the questions. Divide the class into two teams. You'll alternate asking questions to individual members of teams A & B (like in a spelling bee). The question keeps going from A to B until it is correctly answered, then a new question is asked. A correct answer does not allow the team to get another question. Correct answers are +2 points; incorrect answers are -1 point.

4. Allow students time to quiz each other (in pairs) from their study guides and class notes.

5. Give students a crossword puzzle from the Unit Resources section to complete.

REVIEW GAMES / ACTIVITIES

6. Divide your class into two teams. Use the *A Day No Pigs Would Die* crossword words with their letters jumbled as a word list. Student 1 from Team A faces off against Student 1 from Team B. You write the first jumbled word on the board. The first student (1A or 1B) to unscramble the word wins the chance for his/her team to score points. If 1A wins the jumble, go to student 2A and give him/her a clue. He/she must give you the correct word which matches that clue. If he/she does, Team A scores a point, and you give student 3A a clue for which you expect another correct response. Continue giving Team A clues until some team member makes an incorrect response. An incorrect response sends the game back to the jumbled-word face off, this time with students 2A and 2B. Instead of repeating giving clues to the first few students of each team, continue with the student after the one who gave the last incorrect response on the team.

7. Take on the persona of "The Answer Person." Allow students to ask any question about the book. Answer the questions, or tell students where to look in the book to find the answer.

8. Students may enjoy playing charades with events from the story. Select a student to start. Give him/her a card with a scene or event from the story. Allow the players to use their books to find the scene being described. The first person to guess each charade performs the next one.

9. Play a categories-type quiz game. (A master is included in this Unit Plan). Make an overhead transparency of the categories form. Divide the class into teams of three or four players each. Have each team Choose a recorder and a banker. Choose a team to go first. That team will choose a category and point amount. Ask the question to the entire class.(Use the Study Guide Quiz and Vocabulary questions.) Give the teams one minute to discuss the answer and write it down. Walk around the room and check the answers. Each team that answers correctly receives the points. (Incorrect answers are not penalized; they just don't receive any points). Cross out that square on the playing board. Play continues until all squares have been used. The winning team is the one with the most points. You can assign bonus points to any square or squares you choose.

10. Have individual students draw scenes from the book. Display the scenes and have the rest of the class look in their books to find the chapter or section that is being depicted. The first student to find the correct scene then displays his or her picture. When the game is over, collect the pictures and put them in a binder for students to look at during their free time.

NOTE: If students do not need the extra review, omit this lesson and go on to the test.

QUIZ GAME
A Day No Pigs Would Die

Chapters 1-4	Chapters 5-8	Chapters 9-10	Chapters 11-12	Chapters 13-15
100	100	100	100	100
200	200	200	200	200
300	300	300	300	300
400	400	400	400	400
500	500	500	500	500

LESSON NINETEEN

Objective
To test the students' understanding of the main ideas and themes in *A Day No Pigs Would Die*

Activity #1
Distribute the Unit Tests for *A Day No Pigs Would Die*. Go over the instructions in detail and allow the students the entire class period to complete the exam.

Activity #2
Collect all test papers and assigned books prior to the end of the class period.

LESSON TWENTY

Objectives
1. To widen the breadth of students' knowledge about the topics discussed or touched upon in *A Day No Pigs Would Die*
2. To check students' non-fiction assignments

Activity
Ask each student to give a brief oral report about the nonfiction work he/she read for the nonfiction assignment. Your criteria for evaluating this report will vary depending on the level of your students. You may wish for students to give a complete report without using notes of any kind, or you may want students to read directly from a written report, or you may want to do something in between these two extremes. Just make students aware of your criteria in ample time for them to prepare their reports.

Start with one student's report. After that, ask if anyone else in the class has read on a topic related to the first student's report. If no one has, choose another student at random. After each report, be sure to ask if anyone has a report related to the one just completed. That will help keep a continuity during the discussion of the reports.

UNIT TESTS

NOTES ABOUT THE UNIT TESTS IN THIS UNIT:

There are 5 different unit tests which follow.

There are two short answer tests which are based primarily on facts from the novel. The answer key for short answer unit test 1 follows the student test. The answer key for short answer test 2 follows the student short answer unit test 2.

There is one advanced short answer unit test. It is based on the extra discussion questions. Use the matching key for short answer unit test 2 to check the matching section of the advanced short answer unit test. There is no key for the short answer questions. The answers will be based on the discussions you have had during class.

There are two multiple choice unit tests. Following the two unit tests, you will find an answer sheet on which students should mark their answers. The same answer sheet should be used for both tests; however, students' answers will be different for each test. Following the students' answer sheet for the multiple choice tests you will find your answer keys.

The short answer tests have a vocabulary section. You should choose 10 of the vocabulary words from this unit, read them orally and have the students write them down. Then, either have students write a definition or use the words in sentences. The second part of the vocabulary test is matching.

SHORT ANSWER UNIT TEST 1 *A Day No Pigs Would Die*

I. <u>Matching/ Identify</u>

____ 1.	Ben Tanner	A.	town near the Peck farm
____ 2.	Apron	B.	laughed at Rob's confusion
____ 3.	Pinky	C.	pig butcher
____ 4.	Ira Long	D.	Rob delivered her calf
____ 5.	Miss Malcom	E.	died after run-in with a weasel
____ 6.	Learning	F.	Rob's name for his pet
____ 7.	Rutland	G.	sewed up Rob's injured arm
____ 8.	Hussy	H.	owner of a prosperous farm
____ 9.	Haven Peck	I.	Rob went to this fair with the Tanners
____ 10.	Mama	J.	brought his dog to get weaseled

II. <u>Short Answer</u>

1. Describe, in order, the things the narrator did to help Apron.

2. Mr. Peck did not want to accept a gift just for being a good neighbor. How did Mr. Tanner get him to accept the gift?

Short Answer Unit Test 1 *A Day No Pigs Would Die*

3. How did Rob feel the first night he had Pinky?

4. What was Rob's favorite sight?

5. Which day was the day no pigs would die? Why?

Short Answer Unit Test 1 *A Day No Pigs Would Die*

III. <u>Fill-in-the Blank</u>

1. Pinky was growing to be a large pig by November, Papa suspected that she was _____.

2. Mr. Tanner brought _____ to mate with Pinky.

3. The mating was (successful / not successful.)

4. One Saturday in December, Papa _____ Pinky.

5. Rob wanted to _____ and _____ and _____.

6. Instead, he _____.

7. After the deed was finished, Rob said to his father, "Oh, Papa. _____."

8. Papa told Rob that being a man was doing _____.

9. Rob kissed _____.

10. That day was the first time Rob had ever seen his father _____.

IV. <u>Essay</u>

There are several humorous scenes in the book. Summarize one of them. Discuss how the author made the event humorous.

Short Answer Unit Test 1 *A Day No Pigs Would Die*

IV. Vocabulary

Listen to the vocabulary words and spell them. After you have spelled all the words, go back and write down the definitions.

WORD	**DEFINITION**
1.	
2.	
3.	
4.	
5.	
6.	
7.	
8.	
9.	
10.	

Vocabulary Part 2

Directions: Place the letter of the matching definition on the blank line.

____ 1.	provoked	A.	a public showing
____ 2.	spar	B.	strong in body
____ 3.	stout	C.	to awaken
____ 4.	tribulation	D.	nonmetallic light-colored mineral
____ 5.	fret	E.	to solve problems in arithmetic
____ 6.	exhibition	F.	to be uneasy
____ 7.	fester	G.	breeding livestock
____ 8.	cipher	H.	distress; suffering
____ 9.	rouse	I.	to irritate
____ 10.	husbandry	J.	incited to anger or resentment

ANSWER KEY SHORT ANSWER UNIT TEST 1 *A Day No Pigs Would Die*

I. <u>Matching/Identify</u>

H	1.	Ben Tanner	A.	town near the Peck farm
D	2.	Apron	B.	laughed at Rob's confusion
F	3.	Pinky	C.	pig butcher
J	4.	Ira Long	D.	Rob delivered her calf
B	5.	Miss Malcom	E.	died after run-in with a weasel
A	6.	Learning	F.	Rob's name for his pet
I	7.	Rutland	G.	sewed up Rob's injured arm
E	8.	Hussy	H.	owner of a prosperous farm
C	9.	Haven Peck	I.	Rob went to this fair with the Tanners
G	10.	Mama	J.	brought his dog to get weaseled

II. <u>Short Answer</u>

1. Describe, in order, the things the narrator did to help Apron.

    Apron was a Holstein cow who was trying to give birth, but the calf was stuck. The narrator took off his pants and tied one leg around the calf's head. Apron started running again, and he followed her. When she stopped, he tied the other pants leg to a tree. Then he hit and stoned Apron until she started forward, which finally made the calf come out.

    Apron could not breathe. He put his hand down into her throat and felt a hard ball. He pulled on it. The cow bit the narrator's arm and started running. Then the narrator blacked out.

2. Mr. Peck did not want to accept a gift just for being a good neighbor. How did Mr. Tanner get him to accept the gift?

    First, Mr. Tanner asked when Rob's birthday was, then offered the piglet as a late birthday present. Mr. Peck was not comfortable with this. Then Mr. Tanner asked Mr. Peck to help him yoke the two calves the following fall. Mr. Peck agreed and Mr. Tanner offered the piglet as payment. Mr. Peck agreed to this arrangement.

3. How did Rob feel the first night he had Pinky?

    He thought he was the luckiest boy in Learning.

4. What was Rob's favorite sight?

    It was the heavens at sundown.

5. Which day was the day no pigs would die? Why?

    Papa died in his sleep on May third. The neighbors were attending his funeral later that day.

III. Fill-in-the Blank

1. Pinky was growing to be a large pig by November, Papa suspected that she was **barren**.

2. Mr. Tanner brought **Samson** to mate with Pinky.

3. The mating was (successful / **not successful**.)

4. One Saturday in December, Papa **killed/butchered** Pinky.

5. Rob wanted to **run** and **cry** and **scream**.

6. Instead, he **helped his father butcher the pig**.

7. After the deed was finished, Rob said to his father, "Oh, Papa. **My heart's broke**."

8. Papa told Rob that being a man was doing **what had to be done.**

9. Rob kissed **his father's hand, all covered with pig blood**.

10. That day was the first time Rob had ever seen his father **cry**.

IV. Essay Answers will vary, based on the class discussions.

IV. Vocabulary Choose ten words to dictate to your students for part one.

J	1.	provoked	A.	a public showing
D	2.	spar	B.	strong in body
B	3.	stout	C.	to awaken
H	4.	tribulation	D.	nonmetallic light-colored mineral
F	5.	fret	E.	to solve problems in arithmetic
A	6.	exhibition	F.	to be uneasy
I	7.	fester	G.	breeding livestock
E	8.	cipher	H.	distress; suffering
C	9.	rouse	I.	to irritate
G	10.	husbandry	J.	incited to anger or resentment

SHORT ANSWER UNIT TEST 2 *A Day No Pigs Would Die*

I. <u>Matching/ Identify</u>

_____ 1.	Abner Doubleday	A.	Aunt Matty's and the Tanners' religion
_____ 2.	Baptist	B.	Rob removed one from Apron's throat
_____ 3.	Ethan Allen	C.	Mrs. ___ came to the Pecks for help
_____ 4.	Shaker	D.	Peck family religion
_____ 5.	Sebring	E.	Rob thought he was a baseball team captain
_____ 6.	Tanner	F.	local baseball team
_____ 7.	Hillman	G.	Mrs. ___ told Rob to call her Bess
_____ 8.	vote	H.	Rob put his name on a test
_____ 9.	goiter	I.	Mr. Peck couldn't do this, by law
_____ 10.	Greemobys	J.	dug up the coffins

II. <u>Short Answer</u>

1. When did Rob think his father smelled the best, and why?

2. Rob said he disagreed with his father about one Shaker law in particular. What was it? Why did
    he disagree?

Short Answer Unit Test 2 *A Day No Pigs Would Die*

3. What did Mr. Peck say his mission was?

4. After whom was Rob named? Why was this person famous?

5. List, in order, the things Rob did when he got to the fair.

Short Answer Unit Test 2 *A Day No Pigs Would Die*

III. Fill-in-the Blanks
1. *A Day No Pigs Would Die* is an _____.
2. The narrator and author, _____ grew up on a farm in Vermont.
3. His father was a _____.
4. One day at recess, Edward Thatcher _____. Rob got angry and left the schoolyard.
5. On the way home he saw a the Tanners' Holstein cow, named _____.
6. Rob realized that she was about to give birth, but was having difficulty. He managed to tie one end of his _____ around the calf's neck, and the other around a tree. He gave the cow a slap, and the calf was delivered.
7. Then Rob noticed that the cow was having trouble breathing. He put his arm down her throat and pulled out a _____.
8. The cow was so angry she _____.
9. He healed up, and his neighbor gave him a _____ in thanks.
10. Rob named it _____.

IV. Essay
Discuss the significance of the following quotation. Summarize the events that led up to it. "It can't be no longer your mother and Carrie taking care of you. Soon you got to care for them. They're old, too. Years of work done that."

Short Answer Unit Test 2 *A Day No Pigs Would Die*

IV. Vocabulary

Listen to the vocabulary words and spell them. After you have spelled all the words, go back and write down the definitions.

WORD	**DEFINITION**
1.	
2.	
3.	
4.	
5.	
6.	
7.	
8.	
9.	
10.	

Vocabulary Part 2   Directions: Place the letter of the matching definition on the blank line.

_____ 1. smarted   A. a public officer who investigates deaths
_____ 2. pomade   B. people ordained for religious service
_____ 3. hastens   C. pleasing and wholesome in appearance
_____ 4. comely   D. a perfumed hair ointment
_____ 5. prosperous   E. rapid shaking
_____ 6. astir   F. successful
_____ 7. clergy   G. moves or acts swiftly
_____ 8. goad   H. a long stick with a pointed end
_____ 9. quivering   I. caused a stinging pain
_____ 10. coroner   J. moving about

ANSWER KEY SHORT ANSWER UNIT TEST 2 *A Day No Pigs Would Die*

I. <u>Matchig/ Identify</u>
Note: Also use this key for the Advanced Short Answer Unit Test.

H	1.	Abner Doubleday	A.	Aunt Matty's and the Tanners' religion
A	2.	Baptist	B.	Rob removed one from Aprons throat
E	3.	Ethan Allen	C.	Mrs. ___ came to the Pecks for help
D	4.	Shaker	D.	Peck family religion
J	5.	Sebring	E.	Rob thought he was a baseball team captain
G	6.	Tanner	F.	local baseball team
C	7.	Hillman	G.	Mrs. ___ told Rob to call her Bess
I	8.	vote	H.	Rob put his name on a test
B	9.	goiter	I.	Mr. Peck couldn't do this, by law
F	10.	Greemobys	J.	dug up the coffins

II. <u>Short Answer</u>

1. When did Rob think his father smelled the best, and why?
    He smelled the best on Sunday morning, because he had taken a bath on Saturday night and washed the pig smells off. On Sunday he smelled like soap.

2. Rob said he disagreed with his father about one Shaker law in particular. What was it? Why did he disagree?
    He disagreed with the law that said they could not go to baseball games on Sunday. He thought since he would only be watching, it should be acceptable. He wanted to see the Greemobys play.

3. What did Mr. Peck say his mission was?
    He said he mission was killing pigs.

4. After whom was Rob named? Why was this person famous?
    He was named after Major Robert Roger. He was famous because he had done a lot with the Indians. Some of the people thought he was a Shaker.

5. List, in order, the things Rob did when he got to the fair.
    They headed or the stock area. He and Mrs. Tanner looked for a rest room. Next, they went to see Bob and Bib, and get them yoked. They took the oxen to a show area and got their pictures taken. Rob showed the oxen in the exhibition ring. He went to get Pinky and found out she had rolled in manure. He bought a used piece of saddle soap with his dime, and washed her off. He showed Pinky. While showing Pinky, he wiped his head, and the smell of the manure still on his hand made him sick. Just as the judge got to him, he threw up.

II. Fill-in-the Blanks
1. *A Day No Pigs Would Die* is an **autobiography**.
2. The narrator and author, **Robert Newton Peck,** grew up on a farm in Vermont.
3. His father was a **pig butcher.**
4. One day at recess, Edward Thatcher **umade fun of Rob's Shaker ways and clothes.** Rob got angry and left the schoolyard.
5. On the way home he saw a the Tanners' Holstein cow, named **Apron.**
6. Rob realized that she was about to give birth, but was having difficulty. He managed to tie one end of his **trousers** around the calf's neck, and the other around a tree. He gave the cow a slap, and the calf was delivered.
7. Then Rob noticed that the cow was having trouble breathing. He put his arm down her throat and pulled out a **goiter**.
8. The cow was so angry she **bit his arm and dragged him along the ground**.
9. He healed up, and his neighbor gave him a **piglet** in thanks.
10. Rob named it **Pinky**.

III. Essay Answers will vary based on your class discussions.

IV. Vocabulary Choose ten words to dictate to your students for Part 1.

Vocabulary Part 2

I	1.	smarted	A.	a public officer who investigates deaths
D	2.	pomade	B.	people ordained for religious service
G	3.	hastens	C.	pleasing and wholesome in appearance
C	4.	comely	D.	a perfumed hair ointment
F	5.	prosperous	E.	rapid shaking
J	6.	astir	F.	successful
B	7.	clergy	G.	moves or acts swiftly
H	8.	goad	H.	a long stick with a pointed end
E	9.	quivering	I.	caused a stinging pain
A	10.	coroner	J.	moving about

ADVANCED SHORT ANSWER UNIT TEST *A Day No Pigs Would Die*

I. <u>Matching/ Identify</u>

____ 1. Abner Doubleday   A. Aunt Matty's and the Tanners' religion
____ 2. Baptist   B. Rob removed one from April's throat
____ 3. Ethan Allen   C. Mrs. ___ came to the Pecks for help
____ 4. Shaker   D. Peck family religion
____ 5. Sebring   E. Rob thought he was a baseball team captain
____ 6. Tanner   F. local baseball team
____ 7. Hillman   G. Mrs. ___ told Rob to call her Bess
____ 8. vote   H. Rob put his name on a test
____ 9. goiter   I. Mr. Peck couldn't do this, by law
____ 10. Greemobys   J. dug up the coffins

II. <u>Short Answer</u>

1. What are the main conflicts in the story? Are they resolved? If so, how? If not, why not?

2. How did Haven Peck's religious beliefs influence his life?

Advanced Short Answer Unit Test *A Day No Pigs Would Die*

3. The author often used vivid language to describe a scene or event. Give an example of his use of
vivid language that you found most effective. Tell why it was effective.

4. Did Rob's experiences change the way you look at yourself? How?

5. Which senses did the descriptions cause you to use? Give examples of the descriptions using hearing, seeing, touching, smelling, taste.

III. Quotations
    Discuss the significance of the following quotations.
1. "And he wants a fence to divide his and mine, same as I do. He knows this. A fence sets men together, not apart."

Advanced Short Answer Unit Test *A Day No Pigs Would Die*

2. "Course you haven't. Trouble with teachers today is, they don't diagram. All they think of is the
    Bunny Hug."

3. "She don't have folks. They left town after she drown this child, then hung herself. I can't undo
    what's already been did. But the little girl is mine. You hear me, Haven? This child is mine, and I
    claim it soul and dust."

4. "She said I smelled of honest work, and that there was no sorry to be said or heard."

5. "Good night, Papa," I said. "We had thirteen good years."

Advanced Short Answer Unit Test *A Day No Pigs Would Die*

IV. Vocabulary

Listen to the words and write them down. After you have written down all of the words, write a paragraph in which you use all of the words. The paragraph must in some way relate to *A Day No Pigs Would Die*

1. _____
2. _____
3. _____
4. _____
5. _____
6. _____
7. _____
8. _____
9. _____
10. _____

MULTIPLE CHOICE TEST 1 *A Day No Pigs Would Die*

I. Matching/ Identify

____	1. Ben Tanner	A.	town near the Peck farm
____	2. Apron	B.	laughed at Rob's confusion
____	3. Pinky	C.	pig butcher
____	4. Ira Long	D.	Rob delivered her calf
____	5. Miss Malcom	E.	died after run-in with a weasel
____	6. Learning	F.	Rob's name for his pet
____	7. Rutland	G.	sewed up Rob's injured arm
____	8. Hussy	H.	owner of a prosperous farm
____	9. Haven Peck	I.	Rob went to this fair with the Tanners
____	10. Mama	J.	brought his dog to get weaseled

II. Multiple Choice

1. Rob helped Apron. Which of these events is last?
   A. He tied one pants leg to a tree.
   B. He tied one pants leg around the calf's head.
   C. He hit and stoned Apron until she started forward.
   D. Apron started running, and he followed her.

2. Which statement about the animal Mr. Tanner gave Rob is true?
   A. It was a piglet. Rob named it Pinky.
   B. It was a hunting dog. Rob named it Samson.
   C. It was a calf. Rob named it Lil' Apron.
   D. It was a kitten. Rob named it Bib.

3. What, according to Mr. Peck, made Vermont a good state?
   A. Most of the people were Shakers.
   B. The soil was fertile and the taxes were low.
   C. Most of the people were descended from Ethan Allen and the Green Mountain Boys.
   D. The people of Vermont knew they could turn grass into milk and corn into hogs.

4. After whom was Rob named?
   A. He was named after Robert Newton, his mother's father.
   B. He was named after Reverend Henry Robert Peck, a famous Shaker minister.
   C. He was named after Newton Merrill, a Shaker who developed a new way of farming.
   D. He was named after Major Robert Roger, who had done a lot with the Indians.

Multiple Choice Unit Test 1 *A Day No Pigs Would Die*

5. True or False: By June, Pinky was twice as big as Rob.
   A. True
   B. False

6. Aunt Matty had a reason for Rob's D in English. What was it?
   A. She said all he ever thought about was girls.
   B. She said he didn't read enough.
   C. She said the teacher did not explain things well enough.
   D. She said the D was due to his Shaker upbringing

7. What did Rob intend to do with Pinky?
   A. He wanted to show her at fairs and win a lot of money.
   B. He wanted to keep her as a pet.
   C. He wanted her to be a brood sow.
   D. He wanted to trade her for an ox.

8. What did Haven Peck do **first** when he found Sebring Hillman?
   A. He drove them all home for breakfast.
   B. He agreed with Sebring's decision.
   C. He helped Sebring dig in the earth and find the smaller coffin.
   D. He had his gun with him, but said it was for varmints, not neighbors.

9. Which sentence describes the outcome of the pig judging contest for Pinky?
   A. She won a gold ribbon for heaviest pig in her age group.
   B. She was disqualified because she was dirty and smelled like manure.
   C. She did not win a prize, but got a certificate of participation.
   D. She won first prize and a blue ribbon for the best behaved pig.

10. What did Papa tell Rob while they were sitting by the fire in the parlor?
    A. He was going to lose the farm if he didn't pay the mortgage in thirty days.
    B. He and Mama were planning to send Rob to town to go to school.
    C. Mama was going to have another baby.
    D. He knew he was sick and would die within the year.

Multiple Choice Test 1 *A Day No Pigs Would Die*

III. Quotations/ Identify the speaker.
    A. Rob   B. Haven Peck   C. Aunt Matty   D. Mr. Tanner
    E. Mrs. Tanner   F. Sebring Hillman   G. Mama

1. "I don't cotton to raise a fool."

2. "Bob and Bib. And the Bob of it is after you, Robert."

3. "Course you haven't. Trouble with teachers today is, they don't diagram. All they think of is the Bunny Hug."

4. "She don't have folks. They left town after she drown this child, then hung herself. I can't undo what's already been did. But the little girl is mine. You hear me, Haven? This child is mine, and I claim it soul and dust."

5. "Your father. How's his health?"

6. "Good night, Papa. We had thirteen good years."

7. "I'm sure glad to be famed for something."

8. "Hussy, you got more spunk in you than a lot of us menfolk got brains."

9. "And if Iris Bascom and her man giggle in the dark, they can have my blessing for whatever it's worth."

10. "And I'm Bess, from here on."

Multiple Choice Test 1 *A Day No Pigs Would Die*

IV. <u>Vocabulary Part 1</u>   Directions: Place the letter of the matching definition on the blank line.

____ 1. provoked   A. a public showing
____ 2. spar   B. strong in body
____ 3. stout   C. to awaken
____ 4. tribulation   D. nonmetallic light-colored mineral
____ 5. fret   E. to solve problems in arithmetic
____ 6. exhibition   F. to be uneasy
____ 7. fester   G. breeding livestock
____ 8. cipher   H. distress; suffering
____ 9. rouse   I. to irritate
____ 10. husbandry   J. incited to anger or resentment

<u>Vocabulary Part 2</u>   Directions: Underline the word that matches the definition.

11. **with a leg on each side**
    a. comely
    b. fend
    c. astride
    d. partial

12. **kept for producing young**
    a. husbandry
    b. barren
    c. provoked
    d. brood

13. **a plastic or rubber raincoat**
    a. slicker
    b. trunnel
    c. mattock
    d. corset

14. **strong in body**
    a. blundersome
    b. stout
    c. provoked
    d. tribulation

15. **low spirits**
    a. cipher
    b. queer
    c. vapors
    d. barren

16. **a pair of like things**
    a. brace
    b. brood
    c. succotash
    d. goiter

17. **shacks**
    a. vapors
    b. shanties
    c. fester
    d. varmints

18. **to solve problems in arithmetic**
    a. fret
    b. goad
    c. exhibition
    d. cipher

19. **to awaken**
    a. rouse
    b. astir
    c. muzzle
    d. spar

20. **claws of a bird of prey**
    a. talons
    b. brood
    c. fester
    d. hastens

MULTIPLE CHOICE TEST 2 *A Day No Pigs Would Die*

I. <u>Matching/ Identify</u>

____ 1. Abner Doubleday
____ 2. Baptist
____ 3. Ethan Allen
____ 4. Shaker
____ 5. Sebring
____ 6. Tanner
____ 7. Hillman
____ 8. vote
____ 9. goiter
____ 10. Greemobys

A. Aunt Matty's and the Tanners' religion
B. Rob removed one from Apron's throat
C. Mrs. ___ came to the Pecks for help
D. Peck family religion
E. Rob thought he was a baseball team captain
F. local baseball team
G. Mrs. ___ told Rob to call her Bess
H. Rob put his name on a test
I. Mr. Peck couldn't do this, by law
J. dug up the coffins

II. <u>Multiple Choice</u>

1. What did Rob do **first** to help Apron?
    A. He tied one pants leg to a tree.
    B. He tied one pants leg around the calf's head.
    C. He hit and stoned Apron until she started forward.
    D. Apron started running again, and he followed her.

2. True or False: Rob liked the smell his father had on Saturday afternoons.
    A. True
    B. False

3. What was Haven Peck's occupation?
    A. He was a blacksmith.
    B. He was a pig butcher.
    C. He was a minister.
    D. He was a cattle rancher.

4. What did Mr. Tanner give Rob as a gift of thanks for delivering Apron's calf?
    A. He gave Rob one of the calves.
    B. He gave Rob a twenty dollar bill.
    C. He gave Rob a puppy.
    D. He gave Rob a piglet.

Multiple Choice Test 2 *A Day No Pigs Would Die*

5. True or False: Haven Peck could not read or write.
   A. True
   B. False

6. Aunt Matty had a reason for Rob's D in English. What was it?
   A. She said all he ever thought about was girls.
   B. She said he didn't read enough.
   C. She said the teacher did not explain things well enough.
   D. She said the D was due to his Shaker upbringing

7. What was Rob's favorite sight?
   A. It was the heavens at sundown.
   B. It was Pinky in her house.
   C. It was a chocolate cake on the dinner table.
   D. It was his father's smile.

8. What did Haven Peck do **last** when he found Sebring Hillman?
   A. He drove them all home for breakfast.
   B. He agreed with Sebring's decision.
   C. He helped Sebring dig in the earth and find the smaller coffin.
   D. He had his gun with him, but said it was for varmints, not neighbors.

9. Which sentence describes the outcome of the pig judging contest for Pinky?
   A. She won a gold ribbon for heaviest pig in her age group.
   B. She was disqualified because she was dirty and smelled like manure.
   C. She did not win a prize, but got a certificate of participation.
   D. She won first prize and a blue ribbon for the best behaved pig.

10. What did Rob do after he sent his mother and Aunt Carrie to bed with cups of hot tea?
    A. He went to his room and wrote a letter to his father.
    B. He sat by the fire and read the Book of Shaker.
    C. He went out to the orchard to be alone with his father and say goodnight to him.
    D. He broke his father's best knife in anger.

Multiple Choice Test 2 *A Day No Pigs Would Die*

III. Quotations Identify the speaker.

    A. Rob   B. Haven Peck   C. Aunt Matty   D. Mr. Tanner

    E. Mrs. Tanner   F. Sebring Hillman   G. Mama

1. "And if Iris Bascom and her man giggle in the dark, they can have my blessing for whatever it's worth."
2. "No, I cannot read. But our Law has been red to me. And because I could not read, I knew to listen with a full heart. It might be the last and only time I'd learn its meaning."
3. "Next time, I'll teach the pig."
4. "Rob, you feed that pig better than you feed yourself."
5. "She don't have folks. They left town after she drown this child, then hung herself. I can't undo what's already been did. But the little girl is mine. You hear me, Haven? This child is mine, and I claim it soul and dust."
6. "Hussy, you got more spunk in you than a lot of us menfolk got brains."
7. "Papa works all the time. He don't never rest. And worse than that, he works inside himself. I can see it on his face. Like he's been trying all his life to catch up to something. But whatever it is, it's always ahead of him, and he can't reach it."
8. "Your father. How's his health?"
9. "And I'm Bess, from here on."
10. "Good night, Papa. We had thirteen good years."

Multiple Choice Test 2 *A Day No Pigs Would Die*

IV. Vocabulary Part 1   Directions: Place the letter of the matching definition on the blank line.

____ 1. smarted   A. a public officer who investigates deaths
____ 2. pomade   B. people ordained for religious service
____ 3. hastens   C. pleasing and wholesome in appearance
____ 4. comely   D. a perfumed hair ointment
____ 5. prosperous   E. rapid shaking
____ 6. astir   F. successful
____ 7. clergy   G. moves or acts swiftly
____ 8. goad   H. a long stick with a pointed end
____ 9. quivering   I. caused a stinging pain
____ 10. coroner   J. moving about

Vocabulary Part 2   Directions: Circle the letter next to the word that matches the definition.

11. **low spirits**
    a. cipher
    b. queer
    c. vapors
    d. barren

12. **forward, discharging end of a firearm**
    a. passel
    b. silage
    c. shanties
    d. muzzle

13. **to jab or poke with a pointed object**
    a. fend
    b. trunnel
    c. cipher
    d. prod

14. **crossbar with two U-shaped pieces**
    a. trunnel
    b. succotash
    c. prod
    d. yoke

15. **stew of corn, lima beans, and tomatoes**
    a. rouse
    b. capstan
    c. succotash
    d. pomade

16. **claws of a bird of prey**
    a. talons
    b. brood
    c. fester
    d. hastens

17. **fermented green plants**
    a. bracken
    b. silage
    c. shanties
    d. pomade

18. **undesirable people or animals**
    a. varmints
    b. bracken
    c. talons
    d. vapors

19. **undergarment for waist and hips**
    a. tribulation
    b. corset
    c. slicker
    d. mattock

20. **enlargement of the thyroid gland**
    a. bracken
    b. mattock
    c. tribulation
    d. goiter

ANSWER SHEET A Day No Pigs Would Die

Name _____ Date _____ Test # _____

I. Matching   III. Quotations   IV. Vocabulary

1. _____   1. _____   1. _____

2. _____   2. _____   2. _____

3. _____   3. _____   3. _____

4. _____   4. _____   4. _____

5. _____   5. _____   5. _____

6. _____   6. _____   6. _____

7. _____   7. _____   7. _____

8. _____   8. _____   8. _____

9. _____   9. _____   9. _____

10. _____   10. _____   10. _____

                                               Part 2

II. Multiple Choice   11. _____
1. (A) (B) (C) (D)   12. _____
2. (A) (B) (C) (D)   13. _____
3. (A) (B) (C) (D)   14. _____
4. (A) (B) (C) (D)   15. _____
5. (A) (B) (C) (D)   16. _____
6. (A) (B) (C) (D)   17. _____
7. (A) (B) (C) (D)   18. _____
8. (A) (B) (C) (D)   19. _____
9. (A) (B) (C) (D)   20. _____
10. (A) (B) (C) (D)

ANSWER SHEET KEY   Multiple Choice Unit Test 1
A Day No Pigs Would Die

I. Matching

1. H
2. D
3. F
4. J
5. B
6. A
7. I
8. E
9. C
10. G

II. Multiple Choice

1. (A) (B) ( ) (D)
2. ( ) (B) (C) (D)
3. (A) (B) (C) ( )
4. (A) (B) (C) ( )
5. (A) ( ) (C) (D)
6. (A) (B) (C) ( )
7. (A) (B) ( ) (D)
8. (A) (B) (C) ( )
9. (A) (B) (C) ( )
10. (A) (B) (C) ( )

III. Quotations

1. B
2. D
3. C
4. F
5. C
6. A
7. B
8. A
9. G
10. E

IV. Vocabulary

1. J
2. D
3. B
4. H
5. F
6. A
7. I
8. E
9. C
10. G

Part 2
11. C
12. D
13. A
14. B
15. C
16. A
17. B
18. D
19. A
20. A

ANSWER SHEET KEY Multiple Choice Unit Test 2
A Day No Pigs Would Die

I. Matching

1. H
2. A
3. E
4. D
5. J
6. G
7. C
8. I
9. B
10. F

II. Multiple Choice

1. (A) ( ) (C) (D)
2. (A) ( ) (C) (D)
3. (A) ( ) (C) (D)
4. (A) (B) (C) ( )
5. ( ) (B) (C) (D)
6. (A) (B) (C) ( )
7. ( ) (B) (C) (D)
8. ( ) (B) (C) (D)
9. (A) (B) (C) ( )
10. (A) (B) ( ) (D)

III. Quotations

1. G
2. B
3. C
4. G
5. F
6. A
7. A
8. D
9. E
10. A

IV. Vocabulary

1. I
2. D
3. G
4. C
5. F
6. J
7. B
8. H
9. E
10. A

Part 2
11. C
12. D
13. D
14. D
15. C
16. A
17. B
18. B
19. B
20. D

UNIT RESOURCES

BULLETIN BOARD IDEAS

1. Save one corner of the board for the best of students' writing assignments. You may want to use background maps or scenes of Vermont to represent the setting of the novel.

2. Take one of the word search puzzles from the extra activities packet and with a marker copy it over in a large size on the bulletin board. Write the clue words to find to one side. Invite students prior to and after class to find the words and circle them on the bulletin board.

3. Have students find or draw pictures that they think resemble the people in the book.

4. Invite students to help make an interactive bulletin board quiz. Give each student a half-sheet of paper (about 4"x5") folded in half so that it can open. On the outside flap, have each student write a description of one of the characters in the text. On the inside, they will write the name of the character. You can staple or tack these papers to the bulletin board so that the students can read the descriptions and lift the flaps to find the answers.

5. Collect pictures of Vermont farms and Shaker items.

6. Display articles about Robert Newton Peck.

7. Have students design a mural depicting the settings of the book.

EXTRA ACTIVITIES

One of the difficulties in teaching a novel is that all students don't read at the same speed. One student who likes to read may take the book home and finish it in a day or two. Sometimes a few students finish the in-class assignments early. The problem, then, is finding suitable extra activities for students.

One thing that helps is to keep a little library in the classroom. For this unit on *A Day No Pigs Would Die* you might check out from the school or public library other books by Robert Newton Peck. There are also many other similar novels that students would enjoy reading. Several journals have critiques of Peck's works. Some of the students may enjoy reading these and responding either in writing or in discussion groups.

Your students who have reading difficulties, or speak English as a second language may benefit from listening to all or part of the book on tape.

Other things you may keep on hand are word search puzzles. Several puzzles relating directly to *A Day No Pigs Would Die* are included in the unit. Feel free to duplicate them.

Some students may like to draw. You might devise a contest or allow some extra-credit grade for students who draw characters or scenes from *A Day No Pigs Would Die*. Note, too, that if the students do not want to keep their drawings you may pick up some extra bulletin board materials this way. If you have a contest and you supply the prize. You could, possibly, make the drawing itself a non-refundable entry fee.

Have maps, a globe, and travel brochures on hand for easy reference. Travel agencies and automobile clubs are good sources for these materials.

The pages which follow contain games, puzzles, and worksheets. The keys, when appropriate, immediately follow the puzzle or worksheet.

There are two main groups of activities: one group for the unit; that is, generally relating to the text, and another group of activities related strictly to the vocabulary .

Directions for the games, puzzles, and worksheets are self-explanatory. The object here is to provide you with extra materials you may use in any way you choose.

MORE ACTIVITIES

1. Invite a story teller to tell one or more stories related to *A Day No Pigs Would Die* to the class.

2. Use some of the related topics (noted earlier for an in-class library) as topics for research, reports, or written papers, or as topics for guest speakers.

3. Help students design and produce a talk show. Choose one of the story incidents as the topic. The host will interview the various characters. (Students should make up the questions they want the host to ask the characters.)

4. Have students work in pairs to create an interview with one of the characters. One student should be the interviewer and the other should be the interviewee. Students can work together to compose questions for the interviewer to ask. Each pair of students could present their interview to the class.

5. Invite students who have read other books by Robert Newton Peck to present booktalks to the class.

6. Invite students who have read a biography of Robert Newton Peck to tell the class about his life.

7. Invite someone who has lived in Vermont, or who has been a farmer, to speak to the class.

8. Have students hold small group discussions related to topics in the book. Assign a recorder and a speaker for each group. Have the speaker from each group make a report to the class.

9. Invite a speaker from a local 4H club to talk to the class.

Day No Pigs Would Die Word Search

```
P E C K Q V C P H P M L L R P I G S N
N J Z M E X B I D A R M S E F R O D Y
O X T R X M L J T S A P J H F R I A J
M T N R W L Y T A L B P K C X P T I L
O A E E M V Y R C C R N S T T H E S P
L M R A V J C O T T O N T A I L R Y N
O O N D C S M U F T O B N H M E C O J
S X N L R H S S W V D N F T N S R P Z
H B S G E B E K Q E R C N L P O I N Y
Q B H P H A N R B R H R A M A M J N Y
V A A H C R R S Y R X T M L W W A K H
W P K E T R H N E V I D D O L X M Y R
P T E L U E P U I M S N C I N E T A T
T I R P B N H J S N R A G A A T N P W
Q S G S B J Q S K S G L C K R G X L S
V T S L G I C Z K V Y T B O B R R R C
C G R T E Z B J V O J U B G M H I A Y
W H O L S T E I N T R R S A R A H E M
G R E E M O B Y S E B B A S C O M T V
```

ALLEN	CARRIE	JACOB	PIGLET	TANNER
APRON	COTTONTAIL	LEARNING	PIGS	TANNER
ARM	DAISY	LONG	PINKY	TATE
BAPTIST	DIAGRAM	MAJOR	READ	TEACHER
BARREN	GOITER	MALCOM	RUTLAND	THATCHER
BASCOM	GREEMOBYS	MAMA	SAMSON	TROUSERS
BIB	HILLMAN	MATTY	SARAH	VERMONT
BOB	HOLSTEIN	NEWTON	SEBRING	VERNAL
BROOD	HUE	PECK	SHAKER	VOTE
BUTCHER	HUSSY	PHELPS	SOLOMON	

Day No Pigs Would Die Word Search Answer Key

ALLEN	CARRIE	JACOB	PIGLET	TANNER
APRON	COTTONTAIL	LEARNING	PIGS	TANNER
ARM	DAISY	LONG	PINKY	TATE
BAPTIST	DIAGRAM	MAJOR	READ	TEACHER
BARREN	GOITER	MALCOM	RUTLAND	THATCHER
BASCOM	GREEMOBYS	MAMA	SAMSON	TROUSERS
BIB	HILLMAN	MATTY	SARAH	VERMONT
BOB	HOLSTEIN	NEWTON	SEBRING	VERNAL
BROOD	HUE	PECK	SHAKER	VOTE
BUTCHER	HUSSY	PHELPS	SOLOMON	

Day No Pigs Would Die Crossword

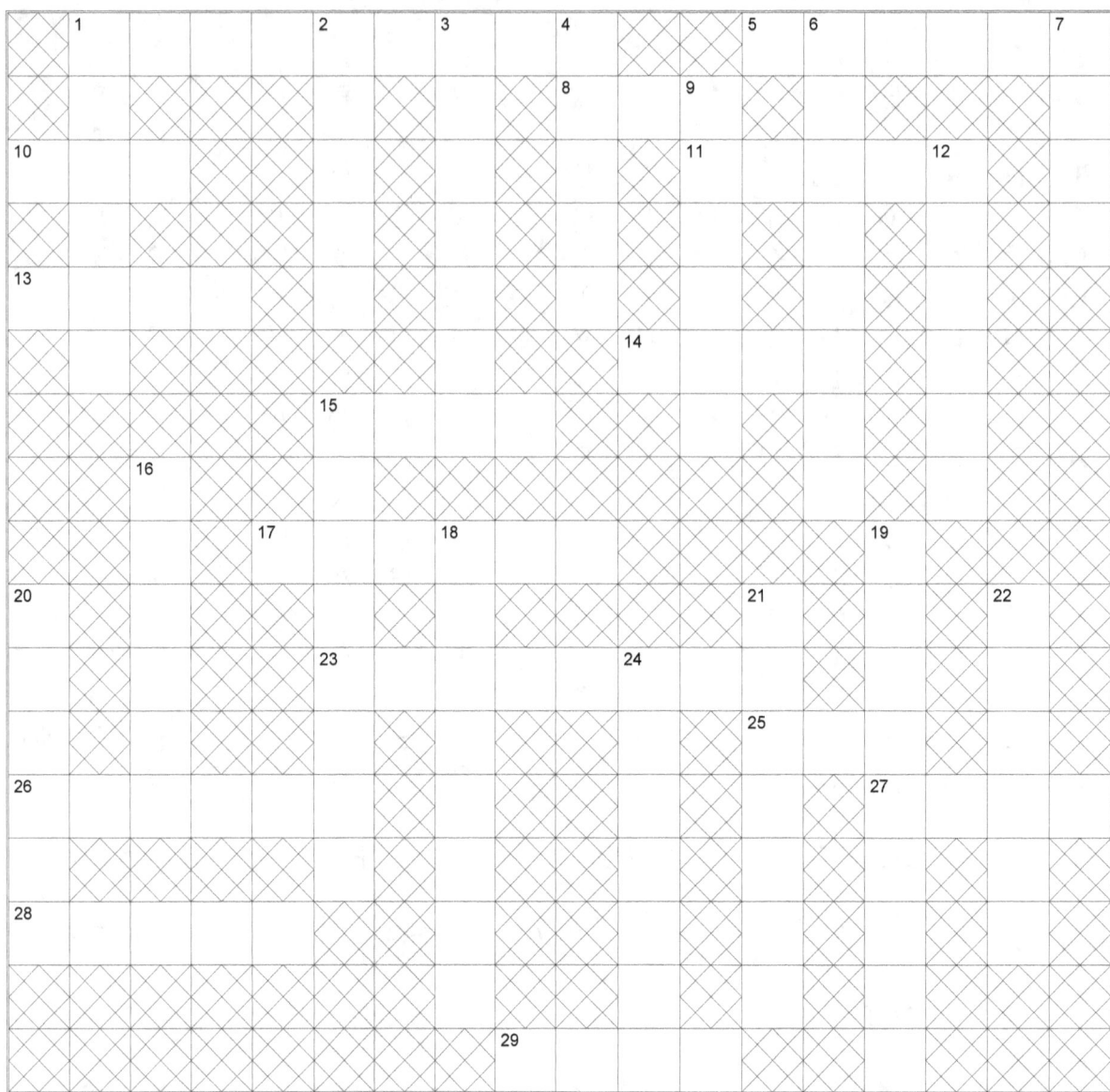

Across
1. Local baseball team
5. Peck family religion
8. injured when Rob helped Apron
10. One of Apron's calves
11. Rob thought Ethan_____was a baseball team captain
13. Pig butcher; Haven_____
14. Mr. Peck couldn't do this, by law
15. Rob looked at Beck_____during meetings
17. Tried to mate with Pinky
23. U.S. President at time of novel; Calvin_____
25. Born due to Rob's efforts
26. Aunt_____thought the Widow Bascom was shameful
27. Ira____ brought his dog to get weaseled
28. Aunt_____tried to teach Rob some grammar
29. Sewed up Rob's injured arm

Down
1. Rob removed one from Apron's throat
2. Rob was named after_____Roger
3. Aunt Matty and the Tanners religion
4. Miss____had kittens in the barn
6. Apron's type of cow
7. Haven Peck was not able to do this
9. Miss____laughed at Rob's confusion
12. Robert_____Peck; narrator
15. Edward_____made fun of Rob
16. Owner of a prosperous farm; Ben_____
18. Poked Rob in the back in class; Will_____
19. Rob put Abner_____'s name on his test
20. Iris_____giggled in the dark with the hired man
21. Dug up the coffins
22. Mrs.____told Rob to call her Bess
24. Ron didn't know how to do this

Day No Pigs Would Die Crossword Answer Key

	1 G	R	E	E	2 M	O	3 B	Y	4 S		5 S	6 H	A	K	E	7 R
	O				A		A		8 A	9 R	M	O				E
10 B	I	B			J		P		R		A	L	L	E	12 N	A
	T				O		T		A		L				E	D
13 P	E	C	K		R		I		H		C				W	
	R						S		14 V	O	T	E			T	
				15 T	A	T	E				M		I		O	
		16 T		H									N		N	
		A	17 S	A	M	18 S	O	N				19 D				
20 B		N		T		T				21 S		O		22 T		
A		N	23 C	O	O	L	I	24 D	G	E		U		A		
S		E	H			D		I		25 B	O	B		N		
26 C	A	R	R	I	E	D		A		R		27 L	O	N	G	
O			R			A		G		I		E		E		
28 M	A	T	T	Y		R		R		N		D		R		
						D		A		G		A				
							29 M	A	M	A		Y				

Across
1. Local baseball team
5. Peck family religion
8. injured when Rob helped Apron
10. One of Apron's calves
11. Rob thought Ethan_____was a baseball team captain
13. Pig butcher; Haven_____
14. Mr. Peck couldn't do this, by law
15. Rob looked at Beck_____during meetings
17. Tried to mate with Pinky
23. U.S. President at time of novel; Calvin_____
25. Born due to Rob's efforts
26. Aunt_____thought the Widow Bascom was shameful
27. Ira____ brought his dog to get weaseled
28. Aunt_____tried to teach Rob some grammar
29. Sewed up Rob's injured arm

Down
1. Rob removed one from Apron's throat
2. Rob was named after_____Roger
3. Aunt Matty and the Tanners religion
4. Miss____had kittens in the barn
6. Apron's type of cow
7. Haven Peck was not able to do this
9. Miss_____laughed at Rob's confusion
12. Robert_____Peck; narrator
15. Edward_____made fun of Rob
16. Owner of a prosperous farm; Ben_____
18. Poked Rob in the back in class; Will_____
19. Rob put Abner_____'s name on his test
20. Iris_____giggled in the dark with the hired man
21. Dug up the coffins
22. Mrs.____told Rob to call her Bess
24. Ron didn't know how to do this

MATCHING QUIZ/WORKSHEET 1 - A Day No Pigs Would Die

___ 1. SARAH   A. One of Apron's calves

___ 2. DOUBLEDAY   B. Mr. Peck couldn't do this, by law

___ 3. MAMA   C. Aunt Matty and the Tanners religion

___ 4. GOITER   D. Apron's type of cow

___ 5. BAPTIST   E. Miss____ had kittens in the barn

___ 6. SHAKER   F. Peck family religion

___ 7. CARRIE   G. Uncle___ was married to Aunt Matty

___ 8. TATE   H. Sewed up Rob's injured arm

___ 9. HUE   I. Owner of a prosperous farm; Ben_____

___ 10. ALLEN   J. Rob thought Ethan_____ was a baseball team captain

___ 11. HOLSTEIN   K. Mrs.____ came to the Pecks for help

___ 12. VOTE   L. Aunt_____ thought the Widow Bascom was shameful

___ 13. HILLMAN   M. Tried to mate with Pinky

___ 14. BUTCHER   N. Gift from Mr. Tanner to Rob

___ 15. MALCOM   O. Pinky's condition

___ 16. LONG   P. Rob removed one from Apron's throat

___ 17. JACOB   Q. Ran through the Widow Bascom's strawberry patch;____ Henry

___ 18. COOLIDGE   R. U.S. President at time of novel; Calvin_____

___ 19. BIB   S. Ira____ brought his dog to get weaseled

___ 20. SAMSON   T. Local baseball team

___ 21. HUSSY   U. Rob looked at Beck_____ during meetings

___ 22. PIGLET   V. Miss____ laughed at Rob's confusion

___ 23. GREEMOBYS   W. Mr. Peck's occupation

___ 24. BARREN   X. Rob put Abner_____'s name on his test

___ 25. TANNER   Y. Died after run-in with a weasel

KEY: MATCHING QUIZ/WORKSHEET 1 - A Day No Pigs Would Die

E - 1.	SARAH	A. One of Apron's calves
X - 2.	DOUBLEDAY	B. Mr. Peck couldn't do this, by law
H - 3.	MAMA	C. Aunt Matty and the Tanners religion
P - 4.	GOITER	D. Apron's type of cow
C - 5.	BAPTIST	E. Miss____ had kittens in the barn
F - 6.	SHAKER	F. Peck family religion
L - 7.	CARRIE	G. Uncle____ was married to Aunt Matty
U - 8.	TATE	H. Sewed up Rob's injured arm
G - 9.	HUE	I. Owner of a prosperous farm; Ben_____
J - 10.	ALLEN	J. Rob thought Ethan_____ was a baseball team captain
D -11.	HOLSTEIN	K. Mrs.____ came to the Pecks for help
B -12.	VOTE	L. Aunt_____ thought the Widow Bascom was shameful
K -13.	HILLMAN	M. Tried to mate with Pinky
W 14.	BUTCHER	N. Gift from Mr. Tanner to Rob
V -15.	MALCOM	O. Pinky's condition
S -16.	LONG	P. Rob removed one from Apron's throat
Q -17.	JACOB	Q. Ran through the Widow Bascom's strawberry patch;_____Henry
R -18.	COOLIDGE	R. U.S. President at time of novel; Calvin_____
A -19.	BIB	S. Ira____ brought his dog to get weaseled
M 20.	SAMSON	T. Local baseball team
Y -21.	HUSSY	U. Rob looked at Beck_____ during meetings
N -22.	PIGLET	V. Miss____ laughed at Rob's confusion
T -23.	GREEMOBYS	W. Mr. Peck's occupation
O -24.	BARREN	X. Rob put Abner_____'s name on his test
I - 25.	TANNER	Y. Died after run-in with a weasel

MATCHING QUIZ/WORKSHEET 2 - A Day No Pigs Would Die

___ 1. MATTY A. Mama didn't mind that Papa smelled like these animals

___ 2. SAMSON B. The Peck's ox

___ 3. PIGS C. Peck family religion

___ 4. COOLIDGE D. Aunt Matty's occupation before marriage

___ 5. HILLMAN E. Mr. Peck couldn't do this, by law

___ 6. BAPTIST F. Dug up the coffins

___ 7. HOLSTEIN G. Mrs.____ told Rob to call her Bess

___ 8. SARAH H. Apron's type of cow

___ 9. BIB I. Local baseball team

___ 10. BROOD J. One of Apron's calves

___ 11. VOTE K. Sewed up Rob's injured arm

___ 12. VERMONT L. Rob put Abner_____'s name on his test

___ 13. GREEMOBYS M. Poked Rob in the back in class; Will_____

___ 14. SHAKER N. Setting of novel

___ 15. PECK O. Tried to mate with Pinky

___ 16. HUE P. injured when Rob helped Apron

___ 17. SEBRING Q. Miss____ had kittens in the barn

___ 18. STODDARD R. Pig butcher; Haven_____

___ 19. TEACHER S. Mrs.____ came to the Pecks for help

___ 20. MAMA T. Aunt____ tried to teach Rob some grammar

___ 21. TANNER U. U.S. President at time of novel; Calvin_____

___ 22. DOUBLEDAY V. Pinky was intended to be a _____ sow

___ 23. LONG W. Ira____ brought his dog to get weaseled

___ 24. ARM X. Uncle___ was married to Aunt Matty

___ 25. SOLOMON Y. Aunt Matty and the Tanners religion

KEY: MATCHING QUIZ/WORKSHEET 2 - A Day No Pigs Would Die

T - 1. MATTY   A. Mama didn't mind that Papa smelled like these animals
O - 2. SAMSON   B. The Peck's ox
A - 3. PIGS   C. Peck family religion
U - 4. COOLIDGE   D. Aunt Matty's occupation before marriage
S - 5. HILLMAN   E. Mr. Peck couldn't do this, by law
Y - 6. BAPTIST   F. Dug up the coffins
H - 7. HOLSTEIN   G. Mrs.____ told Rob to call her Bess
Q - 8. SARAH   H. Apron's type of cow
J - 9. BIB   I. Local baseball team
V -10. BROOD   J. One of Apron's calves
E -11. VOTE   K. Sewed up Rob's injured arm
N -12. VERMONT   L. Rob put Abner_____'s name on his test
I -13. GREEMOBYS   M. Poked Rob in the back in class; Will_____
C -14. SHAKER   N. Setting of novel
R -15. PECK   O. Tried to mate with Pinky
X -16. HUE   P. injured when Rob helped Apron
F -17. SEBRING   Q. Miss____ had kittens in the barn
M -18. STODDARD   R. Pig butcher; Haven____
D -19. TEACHER   S. Mrs.____ came to the Pecks for help
K -20. MAMA   T. Aunt____ tried to teach Rob some grammar
G -21. TANNER   U. U.S. President at time of novel; Calvin_____
L -22. DOUBLEDAY   V. Pinky was intended to be a _____ sow
W 23. LONG   W. Ira____ brought his dog to get weaseled
P -24. ARM   X. Uncle___ was married to Aunt Matty
B -25. SOLOMON   Y. Aunt Matty and the Tanners religion

UNIT WORD SCRAMBLE *A Day No Pigs Would Die*

SCRAMBLE	WORD	CLUE
PRNOA	APRON	Rob delivered her calf
ARECRI	CARRIE	Thought the Widow Bascom was shameful
AYTMT	MATTY	Tried to teach Rob some grammar
APTBTIS	BAPTIST	Aunt Matty's religion
ABRERN	BARREN	Pinky's condition
EBKCY	BECKY	Rob looked at ___ Tate during meetings
ARNTNE	TANNER	Ben ___ owned a prosperous farm
ACTTTOONIL	COTTONTAIL	The hawk caught it
SAIYD	DAISY	The Peck's cow
IADGARM	DIAGRAM	Rob didn't know how to do this
HACTTERH	THATCHER	Edward ___ made fun of Rob
EAHCRTE	TEACHER	Aunt Matty's occupation before marriage
OIETRG	GOITER	Rob removed one from Apron's throat
ANVEH	HAVEN	___ Peck was a pig butcher
ONLSTEHI	HOLSTEIN	Apron's type of cow
UHSYS	HUSSY	Died after run-in with a weasel
EARGLNIN	LEARNING	Town near the Peck farm
PESLPH	PHELPS	Letty ___ killed herself and her baby
ALMMCO	MALCOM	Miss ___ laughed at Rob's confusion
ARHAS	SARAH	Miss ___ had kittens in the barn
ILMHALN	HILLMAN	Mrs. ___ came to the Pecks for help
TNRNAE	TANNER	Mrs. ___ old Rob to call her Bess
IGTPLE	PIGLET	Gift from Mr. Tanner to Rob
PYIKN	PINKY	Rob's name for his pet
UTRNLAD	RUTLAND	Rob went to the ___ Fair
ANMSSO	SAMSON	Tried to mate with Pinky
EBGRSIN	SEBRING	Dug up the coffins
HARKSE	SHAKER	Peck family religion
ONLOSOM	SOLOMON	The Peck's ox
ROTRUSES	TROUSERS	Rob used them to help deliver Apron's calf
EMTVRON	VERMONT	Setting of novel

VOCABULARY RESOURCES

Day No Pigs Would Die Vocabulary Word Search

```
B R O O D C A P S T A N F E S T E R Z
X S T N I M R A V S H M A T T O C K G
C T F W M C K U H T R P B B M Y O S S
L Y S T R D R N C O R O N E R T M E C
E B T J H V E C M Y T U M D F H E I T
R S O Y R L T H D G J Y N Q A V L T H
G J U I E F I A X P G A Y N R D Y N L
Y F T S G N O I T I B I H X E S P A R
G S S A M G G V H S P A H T T L I H T
A A N N L R Q W U O B B R B F T M S R
P F D C L O L H M X N A R R R Q U P I
R M F E N D N A K C M C E A E B Z R B
O A I F D G D S S S I G P C C N Z O U
U L C R S E L T F T A P F E R K L D L
S L D O T B G E T L R X H C T L E F A
E E O D R H T N I V Y I R E E U Q N T
P T P C K S F S J K O R D L R B N M I
Q L C D O Q E U F S K G S E F P K B O
S L I C K E R T L B E V A P O R S Y N
```

ASTIR	COMELY	GOITER	PASSEL	SMARTED
ASTRIDE	CORONER	HASTENS	PAUNCH	SPAR
BARREN	CORSET	HUSBANDRY	POMADE	STOUT
BRACE	EXHIBITION	LOCO	PROD	TALONS
BRACKEN	FARE	MALLET	QUEER	TRIBULATION
BROOD	FEND	MATTOCK	ROUSE	TRUNNEL
CAPSTAN	FESTER	MIRTHFUL	SHANTIES	VAPORS
CIPHER	FRET	MUZZLE	SILAGE	VARMINTS
CLERGY	GOAD	PARTIAL	SLICKER	YOKE

Day No Pigs Would Die Vocabulary Word Search Answer Key

ASTIR	COMELY	GOITER	PASSEL	SMARTED
ASTRIDE	CORONER	HASTENS	PAUNCH	SPAR
BARREN	CORSET	HUSBANDRY	POMADE	STOUT
BRACE	EXHIBITION	LOCO	PROD	TALONS
BRACKEN	FARE	MALLET	QUEER	TRIBULATION
BROOD	FEND	MATTOCK	ROUSE	TRUNNEL
CAPSTAN	FESTER	MIRTHFUL	SHANTIES	VAPORS
CIPHER	FRET	MUZZLE	SILAGE	VARMINTS
CLERGY	GOAD	PARTIAL	SLICKER	YOKE

Day No Pigs Would Die Vocabulary Crossword

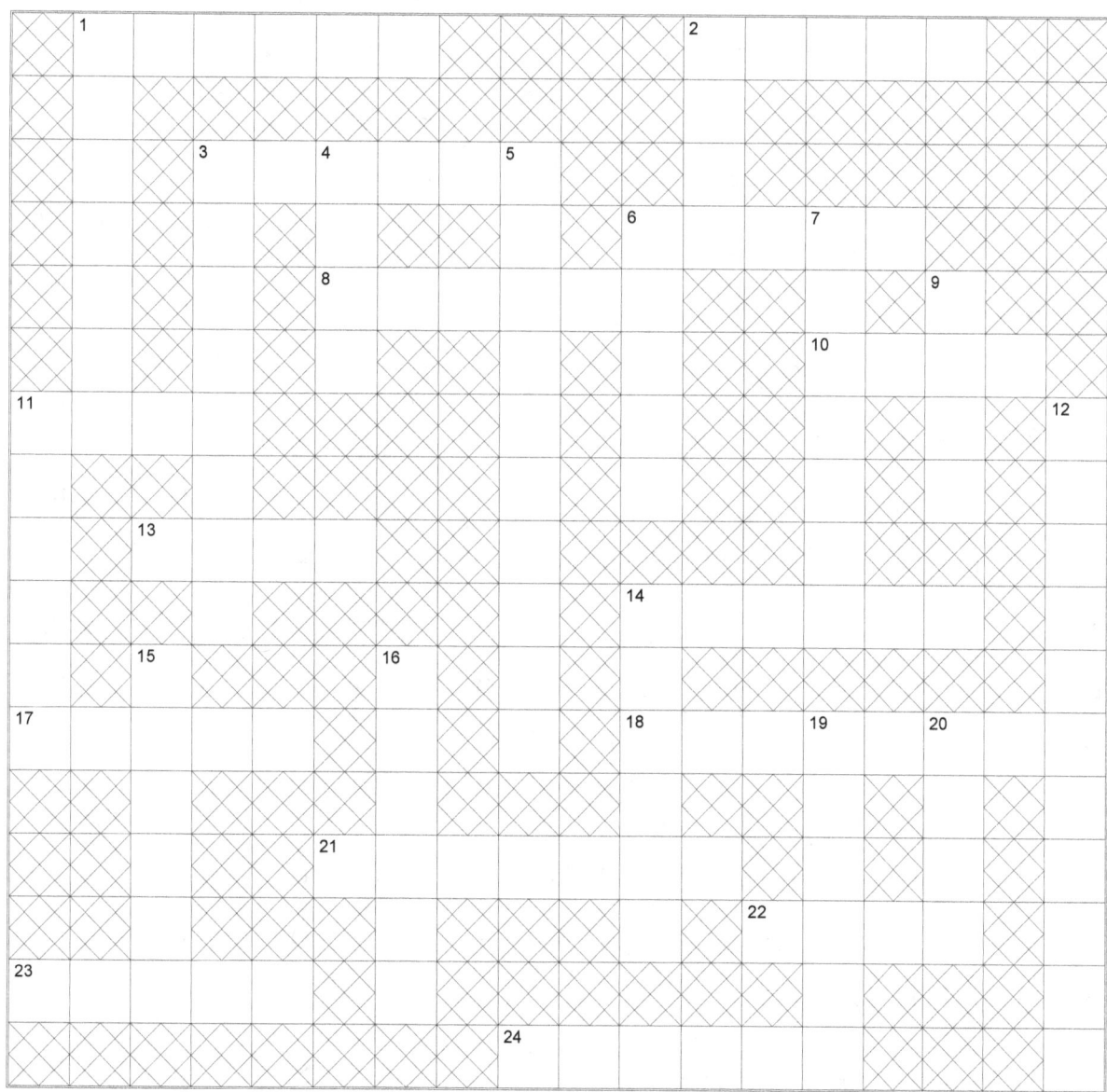

Across
1. Undergarment that supports the waist and hips
2. Strong in body
3. Fermented green plants
6. Pair of like things
8. Solve problems in arithmetic
10. Jab or poke with a pointed object
11. Worry
13. To keep off
14. Potbelly
17. Awaken
18. Full of gladness and gaiety
21. With a leg on each side
22. Crossbar with two U-shaped pieces
23. Strange; odd
24. Low spirits

Down
1. Public officer who investigates deaths
2. Non-metallic light-colored mineral
3. Shacks
4. Mad; insane
5. Public showing
6. Kept for producing young
7. Apparatus used for hoisting weights
9. Long stick with a pointed end
11. Irritate
12. Distress; suffering
14. Perfumed hair ointment
15. The forward, discharging end of the barrel of a firearm
16. Large quantity or group
19. Claws of a bird of prey
20. Get along

Day No Pigs Would Die Vocabulary Crossword Answer Key

Across
1. Undergarment that supports the waist and hips
2. Strong in body
3. Fermented green plants
6. Pair of like things
8. Solve problems in arithmetic
10. Jab or poke with a pointed object
11. Worry
13. To keep off
14. Potbelly
17. Awaken
18. Full of gladness and gaiety
21. With a leg on each side
22. Crossbar with two U-shaped pieces
23. Strange; odd
24. Low spirits

Down
1. Public officer who investigates deaths
2. Non-metallic light-colored mineral
3. Shacks
4. Mad; insane
5. Public showing
6. Kept for producing young
7. Apparatus used for hoisting weights
9. Long stick with a pointed end
11. Irritate
12. Distress; suffering
14. Perfumed hair ointment
15. The forward, discharging end of the barrel of a firearm
16. Large quantity or group
19. Claws of a bird of prey
20. Get along

VOCABULARY MATCHING *A Day No Pigs Would Die*

1. goad
2. silage
3. trunnel
4. tribulation
5. succotash
6. queer
7. pomade
8. passel
9. mirthful
10. mattock
11. exhibition
12. coroner
13. astir
14. blundersome
15. bracken
16. capstan
17. clergy
18. fret
19. husbandry
20. hastens

A. people ordained for religious service
B. moving about
C. a wooden peg that swells when wet
D. a stew of corn, lima beans, and tomatoes
E. fermented green plants
F. causing mistakes
G. a large quantity or group
H. a public showing
I. breeding livestock
J. a public officer who investigates deaths
K. a long stick with a pointed end
L. hair ointment
M. moves or acts swiftly
N. a weedy fern
O. distress; suffering
P. a digging tool with a flat blade
Q. to worry
R. an apparatus used for hoisting weights
S. strange; odd
T. full of gladness and gaiety

ANSWER KEY VOCABULARY MATCHING *A Day No Pigs Would Die*

K	1.	goad	A.	people ordained for religious service
E	2.	silage	B.	moving about
C	3.	trunnel	C.	a wooden peg that swells when wet
O	4.	tribulation	D.	a stew of corn, lima beans, and tomatoes
D	5.	succotash	E.	fermented green plants
S	6.	queer	F.	causing mistakes
L	7.	pomade	G.	a large quantity or group
G	8.	passel	H.	a public showing
T	9.	mirthful	I.	breeding livestock
P	10.	mattock	J.	a public officer who investigates deaths
H	11.	exhibition	K.	a long stick with a pointed end
J	12.	coroner	L.	hair ointment
B	13.	astir	M.	moves or acts swiftly
F	14.	blundersome	N.	a weedy fern
N	15.	bracken	O.	distress; suffering
R	16.	capstan	P.	a digging tool with a flat blade
A	17.	clergy	Q.	to worry
Q	18.	fret	R.	an apparatus used for hoisting weights
I	19.	husbandry	S.	strange; odd
M	20.	hastens	T.	full of gladness and gaiety

VOCABULARY MULTIPLE CHOICE *A Day No Pigs Would Die*

1. **with a leg on each side**
   a. comely
   b. fend
   c. astride
   d. partial

2. **kept for producing young**
   a. husbandry
   b. barren
   c. provoked
   d. brood

3. **a plastic or rubber raincoat**
   a. slicker
   b. trunnel
   c. mattock
   d. corset

4. **strong in body**
   a. blundersome
   b. stout
   c. provoked
   d. tribulation

5. **low spirits**
   a. cipher
   b. queer
   c. vapors
   d. barren

6. **pleasing, wholesome appearance**
   a. astir
   b. fare
   c. comely
   d. prosperous

7. **a long stick with a pointed end**
   a. fend
   b. goad
   c. cipher
   d. paunch

8. **crossbar with two U-shaped pieces**
   a. trunnel
   b. succotash
   c. prod
   d. yoke

9. **a pair of like things**
   a. brace
   b. brood
   c. succotash
   d. goiter

10. **shacks**
    a. vapors
    b. shanties
    c. fester
    d. varmints

11. **to solve problems in arithmetic**
    a. fret
    b. goad
    c. exhibition
    d. cipher

12. **to awaken**
    a. rouse
    b. astir
    c. muzzle
    d. spar

13. **claws of a bird of prey**
    a. talons
    b. brood
    c. fester
    d. hastens

14. **fermented green plants**
    a. bracken
    b. silage
    c. shanties
    d. pomade

15. **undesirable people or animals**
    a. varmints
    b. bracken
    c. talons
    d. vapors

16. **undergarment that supports waist and hips**
    a. tribulation
    b. corset
    c. slicker
    d. mattock

ANSWER KEY VOCABULARY MULTIPLE CHOICE *A Day No Pigs Would Die*

1. with a leg on each side
    a. comely
    b. fend
    c. *astride*
    d. partial

2. kept for producing young
    a. husbandry
    b. barren
    c. provoked
    d. *brood*

3. a plastic or rubber raincoat
    a. *slicker*
    b. trunnel
    c. mattock
    d. corset

4. strong in body
    a. blundersome
    b. *stout*
    c. provoked
    d. tribulation

5. low spirits
    a. cipher
    b. queer
    c. *vapors*
    d. barren

6. pleasing, wholesome appearance
    a. astir
    b. fare
    c. *comely*
    d. prosperous

7. a long stick with a pointed end
    a. fend
    b. *goad*
    c. cipher
    d. paunch

8. crossbar with two U-shaped pieces
    a. trunnel
    b. succotash
    c. prod
    d. *yoke*

9. a pair of like things
    a. *brace*
    b. brood
    c. succotash
    d. goiter

10. shacks
    a. vapors
    b. *shanties*
    c. fester
    d. varmints

11. to solve problems in arithmetic
    a. fret
    b. goad
    c. exhibition
    d. *cipher*

12. to awaken
    a. *rouse*
    b. astir
    c. muzzle
    d. spar

13. claws of a bird of prey
    a. *talons*
    b. brood
    c. fester
    d. hastens

14. fermented green plants
    a. bracken
    b. *silage*
    c. shanties
    d. pomade

15. undesirable people or animals
    a. *varmints*
    b. bracken
    c. talons
    d. vapors

16. undergarment that supports waist and hips
    a. tribulation
    b. *corset*
    c. slicker
    d. mattock

VOCABULARY WORD SCRAMBLE *A Day No Pigs Would Die*

Scrambled	Word	Definition
SRATI	ASTIR	moving about
TESRAID	ASTRIDE	with a leg on each side
BRNRAE	BARREN	not able to produce offspring
RAEBC	BRACE	a pair of like things
RCNABKE	BRACKEN	a weedy fern
RDOBO	BROOD	kept for producing young
ACPNTAS	CAPSTAN	an apparatus used for hoisting weights
IRCHPE	CIPHER	to solve problems in arithmetic
LEYRCG	CLERGY	people ordained for religious service
OMYCEL	COMELY	pleasing and wholesome in appearance
OCRRONE	CORONER	a public officer who investigates deaths
ORECST	CORSET	undergarment that supports waist and hips
EFRSTE	FESTER	irritate
OIRGTE	GOITER	an enlargement of the thyroid gland
SHSATEN	HASTENS	moves or acts swiftly
ATLMLE	MALLET	a short-handled hammer with a large head
AMTKOTC	MATTOCK	a digging tool with a flat blade
IFRTULHM	MIRTHFUL	full of gladness and gaiety
UZEMZL	MUZZLE	discharging end of the barrel of a firearm
ALRTPIA	PARTIAL	having a liking or fondness for
SLASPE	PASSEL	a large quantity or group
APHUNC	PAUNCH	a potbelly
OPDMAE	POMADE	a large quantity or group
UREQE	QUEER	strange; odd
UQIGVREIN	QUIVERING	rapid shaking
OEURS	ROUSE	to awaken
HSASNIET	SHANTIES	shacks
IGLSAE	SILAGE	fermented green plants
LCSIEKR	SLICKER	a plastic or rubber raincoat
MSDARET	SMARTED	caused a stinging pain
SOTTU	STOUT	strong in body
SALTNO	TALONS	claws of a bird of prey
RTULNEN	TRUNNEL	a wooden peg that swells when wet
APRVOS	VAPORS	low spirits
RAMSVINT	VARMINTS	things that are undesirable or troublesome

www.ingramcontent.com/pod-product-compliance
Lightning Source LLC
Chambersburg PA
CBHW051411070526
44584CB00023B/3375